Libby Hoffman

D0960221

Also by Chris Offutt

Out of the Woods

The Good Brother

The Same River Twice

Kentucky Straight

No Heroes

A Memoir of Coming Home

Chris Offutt

SIMON & SCHUSTER
New York London Toronto Sydney Singapore

SIMON & SCHUSTER
Rockefeller Center
1230 Avenue of the Americas
New York, New York 10020

Copyright © 2002 by Chris Offutt
All rights reserved, including the right of reproduction
in whole or in part in any form.

SIMON & SCHUSTER
and colophon are registered trademarks
of Simon & Schuster Inc.

For information about special discounts for bulk purchases,
please contact Simon & Schuster Special Sales:
1-800-456-6798 or business@simonandschuster.com

Designed by Katy Riegel
Manufactured in the United States of America
1 3 5 7 9 10 8 6 4 2

Library of Congress Cataloging-in-Publication Data is available.

ISBN 0-684-86551-3

To Mrs. Jayne,
my first-grade teacher

A place belongs forever
to whoever claims it hardest,
remembers it most obsessively,
wrenches it from itself,
shapes it, renders it, loves it
so radically that he remakes it
in his own image.

—Joan Didion

Portions of this book appeared in various forms in *The New York Times Sunday Magazine, River Teeth, ACE Magazine,* and *OK You Mugs.*

For providing time and space to work, the author wishes to thank Yaddo and Minnow.

No Heroes

Prologue

No matter how you leave the hills—the army, prison, marriage, a job—when you move back after twenty years, the whole county is carefully watching. They want to see the changes that the outside world put on you. They are curious to know if you've lost your laughter. They are worried that perhaps you've gotten above your raisings.

To reassure the community, you should dress down except when you have to dress up, then wear your Sunday-go-to-meeting clothes. Make sure you drive a rusty pickup that runs like a sewing machine, flies low on the straight stretch, and hauls block up a creek bed. Hang dice from the mirror and a gun rack in the back window. A rifle isn't necessary, but something needs to be there—a pool cue, a carpenter's level, an ax handle. Where the front plate should be, screw one on that says "American by birth, Kentuckian by the grace of God."

Be polite to everybody. Even if you are certain you have never seen this lady in your life, ask how her family is. No matter that this man once tore you up one side and down the other, the worst skull-dragging in county history, let bygones be bygones. Smile and nod, smile and nod. When a conversation ends, always say "See you in church."

Tell them it's a big world out there. The desert is hotter than Satan's Hades. The Rocky Mountains are higher than our hills. The ocean is polluted, cities smell bad, and a working man never gets ahead. Don't talk about the beautiful people in stylish clothes. Never mention museums, the opera, theater, and ethnic restaurants. Forget the time you visited a movie star in his home, drank a thousand-dollar bottle of wine, or rode all over Chicago in a limo. That sunset walk across the Brooklyn Bridge doesn't hold a candle to crossing Lick Fork Creek on a one-man swaying bridge. Fine dining will make you fat, but fresh butter on corn bread will make you cry.

Take home as many books as you can. Every bookstore at home for fifty miles is heavy on cookbooks, mysteries, and romance, but a little short on poetry. Remember, poetry in the hills is found, not written. It lies in the handles of tools passed down through families, an ax sharpened so many times the blade is the size of a pocketknife.

Bring palpable evidence of where you've been. Take back objects to hold and smell—no photographs. Take back a stuffed possum, subway tokens, a hockey puck, petrified rock, a porcupine quill, a buffalo hide. Be prepared at all times to say it's better here. You spent twenty years trying to get out of Rowan County and twenty more trying to get back.

Before you leave the city, don't forget to borrow CDs from your friends and make copies of music no radio plays and no store sells. Jazz in the hills is a verb, and pop is what you drink. The Motown sound is a sweet rumble made by muscle cars. Soul is the province of the preacher, and the blues is what going to town will fix. Remember, you won't ever get tired of sitting on the back porch facing the woods with a group of people playing banjo, guitar, mandolin, and fiddle. They will make music through dusk and into the night, a sound so sweet the songbirds lie down and die.

Now that you've got a houseful of what you can't get, think about what you don't need anymore. Best left behind is the tuxedo. You'll never wear it here. May as well trade your foreign car for American if you want to get it worked on. You'll not need burglar alarms, bike locks, or removable car stereo systems. The only gated community is a pasture. The most important things you can get rid of are the habits of the outside world. Here, you won't get judged by your jeans and boots, your poor schooling, or your country accent. Never again will you worry that you're using the wrong fork, saying the wrong thing, or expecting people to keep their word. Nobody here lies except the known liars, and they're great to listen to.

No more will you need to prove your intelligence to bigots. You can go ahead and forget all your preplanned responses to comments about wearing shoes, the movie *Deliverance,* indoor plumbing, and incest. You don't have to work four times as hard because the boss expects so little. You don't have to worry about waiting for the chance to intellectually ambush some nitwit who thinks you're stupid because of where you're from.

You won't hear these words spoken anymore: redneck, hillbilly, cracker, stump-jumper, weed-sucker, ridge-runner. Never again will you have to fight people's attempts to make you feel ashamed of where you grew up. You are no longer from somewhere. Here is where you are. This is home. This dirt is yours.

Job Interview

Kentuckians have a long tradition of going west for a new life and winding up homesick instead. Some went nuts, some got depressed, and some made do. I did a little of all three, then got lucky. I finagled an interview for a teaching position at the only four-year university in the hills. It was more of a high school with ashtrays than a genuine college. I should know. Twenty years ago I graduated from there.

Morehead State University began as a Normal School to produce teachers for the Appalachian region, then progressed to college status. During the 1960s it became a full-fledged university, but natives still referred to it as "the college." Very few local people attended MSU. I had gone to grade school, high school, and college within a ten-mile radius. It wasn't until much later that I understood how unusual this was, particularly in such a rural environment.

As a theater and art student I supported myself by working part-time for the MSU Maintenance Department. Few of my fellow workers had finished high school and none had gone to college. According to hill culture, you were a sinner or an outlaw, a nice girl or a slut, lived with your folks or got married, worked at maintenance or went to college. This either/or mentality is a product of geography. Land here is either slanted or not, and you lived on a ridge or in a hollow. That I was simultaneously engaged in both attending college and working at maintenance astonished my coworkers and faculty alike.

I worked on the painting crew specializing in the outdoor jobs no one else wanted. Many times I painted a curb yellow in the morning, then stepped over it on my way to class that afternoon. Teachers ignored me when I wore my work clothes. My maintenance buddies felt uncomfortable if they saw me going to class, and I developed the habit of eating alone to conceal the book in my lunch bucket. Now I was back to interview for a job as an English teacher.

Before the interview I borrowed a tie from Clyde James, a man who'd been my neighbor and baby-sitter when I was four years old. He now ran the MSU student center. Clyde was something of a clothes horse, and rumor had it that his closets were carefully organized so that he didn't wear the same outfit twice per year. My lack of a tie was no surprise to Clyde, who was delighted to assist me. After narrowing his choices to three, he picked a tie that vaguely matched my slick clothes—dark pants, light shirt, tan jacket. I'd bought a brown belt for the occasion, my single concession to formal dress. Clyde thought brown shoes would have been better than black, but I could pass. He deftly tied a half-Windsor knot, looped it beneath my collar, and adjusted it to a snug fit. The material was blue and gray silk, with a touch of red—perfectly conservative. He smoothed my collar and sent me out, calling me "Prof Offutt."

As I left the building, two maintenance men emerged from a basement door of the student center. Flecks of dry paint spattered their clothes. They leaned against the wall and lit cigarettes just as I had done twenty years before. The basement door was partially concealed by a wall that rose five feet to street level. It was the ideal hidey-hole, a bunker from which you could spy a boss in plenty of time to return to work.

"Hey boys," I said. "Working hard?"

"Hidy, Chris," the younger man said. "Ain't seen you in a while."

"Is that Awful Offutt?" the other said. "By God he's growed, ain't he. Want a cigarette?"

I shook my head. Men of the hills don't have the custom of shaking hands or hugging or cheek-kissing. We either beat on each other or look away and mumble. I had known the younger man all my life. Otis was from Haldeman, my home hill of two hundred people.

"How's your mom and dad?" he said.

"They're all right. And yours?"

"Same. I see your mom in town, but your daddy don't hardly leave the house, does he."

"Not much," I said.

"What's he do?"

"You'll have to ask him."

The older man was named Billy. We worked together twenty years before, and he had mistakenly believed that I sought the salaried maintenance position he coveted. Billy was my age but looked fifteen years older. His palms were the most heavily callused I'd ever seen.

"Kenny still boss?" I said.

"He died," Billy said.

"Big Bob?"

"Retired."

"How about that Johnson?"

"Which one?"

"From up Christy Creek," I said. "Used to drink a half-pint before lunch."

"Oh, him. He's in the state pen."

"Well, ain't there nobody still yet there?"

"Me."

"You must be the boss man now."

"Naw," Billy said. His voice took on the angry tone I remembered. "They gave it to somebody else. What are you doing back? Going to court?"

"No, why?"

He lifted his chin in a gesture toward my tie.

"You're dressed for it."

"These are my job-hunting clothes."

Otis grinned at me. Within the contours of his face I saw the child I recalled from our shared time playing in the woods. We knew the secrets of each other's scars.

"You coming back?" he said.

"Trying to. I got an interview today."

"Where at?"

"The college."

"They're hiring," Otis said. "I don't know if you can get on with the painters, but they need movers. You go in there and talk to Amos Riddle. You know any Riddles? They live up on Redbird."

"It's not for maintenance, Otis."

"It's not."

"No," I said. "It's for teaching. You know, to be a teacher."

Otis and Billy erupted with laughter, bellowing as if

their lives lacked mirth and they were grateful for the joke. When the sound trailed away, they looked at me and I knew they were waiting for the truth.

"I swear, boys," I said. "I took it up out west."

"Awful Offutt ain't changed a bit, has he," Billy said as he laughed again.

"You should have heard him when he was little," Otis said. "He told us there was a whale under the grade school."

"I didn't know any better."

"What I want to know," Billy said, "is who told you they were hiring maintenance men to teach college?"

They began to laugh again, their breath coming hard before shifting to smokers' rasping. They calmed themselves, glanced at each other, and began to giggle.

"Hey," Otis said. "Maybe you can put in a word for me. I'd like to be the boss of a girls' dorm. One of them live-ins."

"All right," I said. "How about you, Billy?"

"I'll take president. Then I can fire you for lying."

"I ain't lying, boys."

"The truth has got to be in him," Otis said. "Because it ain't never come out yet."

"What time is it," I said. "I got that interview at nine o'clock."

"Now I know you're lying," he said. "It's five after."

He showed me his watch, and I hurried away, their laughter hanging in the air like pollen. I understood Billy and Otis's consternation at my being a teacher. As a student in the seventies, I was usually stoned on marijuana. My work strategy had been to complete my task at a furious speed, then rest until quitting time. Neither Otis nor Billy had any reason to believe I had changed. That any maintenance worker, particularly one with my habits, could become a teacher confirmed all their fears and suspicions about the university. B.A. stood for "Big Asshole," B.S. stood for "Bull Shit," and Ph.D. stood for "Piled High and Deep." At MSU the wisest people worked for maintenance and the stupidest had the most letters after their name.

College teachers were rich, snobby, and dumber in the head than a hog is in the ass. The good one was rare, yet untrustworthy, like a dog that licked your hand but had a history of biting. The administrators were worse—bigwigs who possessed more money than God and were utterly corrupt. They served as further evidence that education was for fools. Part of my coming home was meant to contradict this hill-bred belief.

I crossed the street to the Combs building, a small structure that housed the Departments of English, Philosophy, Foreign Languages, and Theater. The curbs were faded yellow and needed a fresh coat. I faced the reflective glass of the door and adjusted the tie around my neck. No matter how I tried, it wasn't as good as when Clyde tied it for me and I looked like what I was—a curb painter in a monkey suit.

Inside, I met the head of the search committee moving in that rapid way professors have, legs propelling her forward, one hand digging in a briefcase, the other hand trying to catch a pencil as it fell from behind her ear.

"Sorry I'm late," she said. "These things never start on time."

"No problem," I said. "I was just, you know."

"Yes, it must be kind of . . ."

"It sure is."

"I understand."

She led me along the hall. A part of me wanted to run away, but this was where I'd run to. The interview was conducted in the same classroom where I'd taken freshman literature twenty years earlier. The floor was now carpeted but the walls were still concrete block. Six people sat in spongy chairs surrounding two wooden tables. I looked at the men in brown jackets and sport shirts, the women in pantsuits, and understood that I was sitting before a table of career academics who found themselves at a lousy school. They lived in an Appalachian town of six thousand with no airport, no bookstore, no deli, no record store, one bar, and forty churches. Everyone but me had a Ph.D. Unlike them, I truly wanted to work at MSU.

My main desire was an opportunity to give back to the community. I knew the difficulties that young people in the hills faced in realizing their ambition of education. My goal was to teach writing in a region where thirty percent of the people were functionally illiterate.

I sat at the table and answered the questions while looking through the window at the basement hidey-hole of Otis and Billy. They had risen to the ranks of salaried maintenance men with intimate knowledge of how to appear industrious—the equivalent of academic tenure. I suddenly wished I was interviewing to work with them. This astounded me to the point of tears, and I heard my voice stop talking. My eyes blinked and the faculty faces blurred. The interview ended slowly, like batteries running down in a mechanical toy. The head of the search committee led me out.

"Good job," she said. "You clinched it when you got choked up. We're not used to seeing someone care about teaching that much."

I followed her to brief meetings with various administrators. MSU has a lovely setting with high hills as a backdrop to the buildings. Spring's pastel trees were patched dark where the sun hit. I remembered hours throwing Frisbees here. We wore shabby clothes, protested disco music, and mourned Lynyrd Skynyrd. My wallet contained rolling papers instead of money. We felt free. Now I felt like an impostor, the butt of a colossal group joke. Any minute someone would say: "Just kidding, Chris. We don't hire locals or ex–curb painters. Now get the hell out of here."

Walking the length of campus took ten minutes, and I headed back along Main Street, looking at the hills silhouetted against the sky. These woods were the cradle of my personal civilization, my own promised land. I grew up walking the same dirt for sixteen years, then began driving it. Town was where the groceries were, the doctor and the drugstore. Town was special. Town was exciting. Town was a half hour's drive on a narrow road that followed a creek. I recalled each incarnation of a restaurant now converted to apartments. Stores were gone, but their sites were forever known to locals as "where Allen's used to be," or "Parney's old place." Directions to newcomers were disastrous—"Drive up Main past the old post office and turn where Bishop's was, I don't know the name of the street, then head down to where they've got that new stuff going on. Park by the old Big Store." Directions in the hills were just as confusing—"Go out sixty past the wide place, go left at the creek, go three hollers up and make a right. If you hit Sharkey, you've gone about twenty miles too far, but there's no sign for it. You'll just know."

A car slowed beside me. The smiling driver was a wild friend from college, now transformed into a straitlaced pillar of the community. She had not only quit her outlaw ways, but she now behaved as if her past belonged to someone else. She drove me ten miles out of town to see a house. I asked Vondelle about various mutual friends, some dead, some vanished, most reformed. A few still lived as we had, managing to maintain a dope and whiskey lifestyle while pursuing careers and having families, although the "plumb wald" times were relegated to weekend parties, where cops hid on old dirt lanes waiting to arrest people as they left. Knowing the backroads was still crucial to living here.

"I spent all these years away dreaming of coming home," I said.

"I spent the same years thinking about leaving."

"It's easy to leave."

"Not for me," Vondelle said. "This is where I went to. Nobody in my family finished high school. I came here for college."

She had married the most exotic man available, an artist from off, which meant beyond the county line. He had no people. No one knew his history. He dropped into the hills fully formed and self-contained, like trailers on a ridge. Without a past, he had no enemies, no fears, no obligations. Vondelle had been a hippie artist from a tough county, full of confidence and glee at living in Morehead, eastern Kentucky's den of iniquity. She liked to laugh, and party hardy. She had been resplendent with the enthusiasm of youth, determined to leave her mark. These days Vondelle and her husband no longer made art.

She turned onto a side road and began driving uphill, taking two turns past a large pond that shimmered in the sun. A duck skidded to a halt beside a cluster of cattails. Birds made a symphony in the trees. She drove slowly up a steep road to a large house. The property included two outbuildings and a section of a wooded hill. We walked along the front slope covered with butterweed and larkspur swaying below white oaks.

I told her I wanted to be alone and she nodded. Redbud blossoms hazed the hills, specked in spots by dogwood. My mouth felt dry and my heart beat fast. For the first time in five years I stepped into the woods. The smell of fresh earth was instantly calming. A pair of sparrows chased a jay. Everything was familiar—the scent, the sight, the light, the dirt.

I walked into the woods and sat on a wind-felled tree a few feet off the ground, a massive hickory rotten through the guts. A pileated woodpecker swam the air, a black and white swirl that landed on a dead maple. It scaled ten feet of trunk in three-step hops, probing the bark for food. I tipped my head to watch and my weight shifted and I fell backward. I gripped the bark tightly but could not fully regain stability. The strength in my arms began to wane beneath the inexorable pull of the earth. The bark scraped my sleeves as I eased my head to the ground, feet aimed at the sky. After five minutes in the woods, I was upside down.

I began to laugh, which caused me to tip until my legs

crashed into the undergrowth. I curled instinctively to an infant's posture of the womb, my eyes inches from last year's leaves. My laughter subsided to a ragged breathing. I surrendered to the years of stifled yearning, weeping with relief at lying alone in the woods of home.

Time seemed to bend as if pressing a nail to a sheet of plastic until it punctured and I entered the intervening space. I had always lain here. I had never abandoned Kentucky. There was no pattern of departure and return, only the seasonal cycle of death and life. Yesterday I had left winter in the west and traveled to spring, a time of hope and portent. The hills flourished with energy. I could smell the moldering decay and the fresh buds twining in one scent. Beside my face an acorn's slender tendril aimed toward the sky, a thin root tethering it to earth. A sense of contentment passed through me like the hint of summer rain. I had no mind, no thought.

Eventually the chill of the earth revived me and I sat, feeling as if I had fallen into my heart. Beneath a leaf I found a morel, pale as a minnow. It needed a week of sun and rain to draw it through the leaves. In a month it would be rotted black. I looked about the woods and vowed to return before the mushroom died. As if in answer, a breeze slid along the lower boughs.

I walked out of the woods to the car, where Vondelle sat. "I'm buying this place," I said.

There was a sadness to her expression, as if she wished she were emerging from the woods with a tear-streaked face and a sense of certainty. She had two sons, the same as me, but hers were a decade older. This was a house for young boys to grow up in, not teenagers to leave. I understood that she brought me to the house precisely because she couldn't have it, as if her knowledge of its availability was a welcoming gift. Vondelle dropped me in Morehead near the realtor's office.

Town culture is taciturn and guarded while giving the impression of being open and friendly. Lives are ruined by a chance encounter in a grocery store parking lot, during which one person didn't notice a neighbor, who felt hurt by the slight. People driving by gave me the Morehead Stare—a long sideways gaze. Originally a response to being part of a small town, where you looked at everyone carefully to see if you should wave or not, the Morehead Stare had blossomed into tradition. The best response was to wave at everyone.

The realtor and I spent a few minutes asking each other about our families. I told him about the house and wrote a check for earnest money. The realtor was surprised that I could buy a house without stepping inside. He said that his wife would never let him do that. I told him we had rented our last four houses over the phone. Each time we arrived with our fingers crossed in a rental truck. He shook his head in an incredulous fashion. He'd lived all his life in Morehead, worked in the family business, and was engaged in politics. As a child I had envied the privilege of his family, and now he envied my travels. Our lives had arced into equality—we were both Rowan Countians of the age when men accumulate power, forge alliances, and run towns. We were educated locals, a scarce commodity in the hills.

I stepped outside and spoke briefly to a man I remembered from high school. I vaguely recalled something bad about him, but I could not trust the memory because Morehead thrived on innuendo, scuttlebutt, and outright lies. When I was a kid Rowan County had telephone party lines that included two to eight families. No conversation was private. The telephone functioned primarily as a method of disseminating information to all the eavesdroppers along the ridge. Gossip was the mortar that held Morehead together. Everyone lived downstream of rumor.

I entered the bank through doors I'd opened a thousand times—first with my mother, then later on my own. Thirty years ago I began a savings account here, depositing a dollar a week until I bought a bicycle. Now I sat in a fake vinyl chair and smiled politely at the employees. Out west I was one of the perpetual faces with no history, a drifter, a stranger, a man from the east. Here everyone knew my entire line—root, branch, and fork.

Wearing blue jeans in the bank meant I was a local. The

gray in my hair meant I'd been away. My very presence meant I sought money. By the end of the day, word of my impending return would spread throughout the county. Some stories would have me moving in with my folks because one of them was very sick. Another had me purchasing my old grade school and converting it to an art colony. I was living in a houseboat on Cave Run Lake. I had AIDS and came home to die. My wife had left me and I was back to hunt another. One story said it wasn't Chris Offutt but his younger brother who was investing in the new mall. When the truth finally outed, everyone knew I was not living where I grew up in Haldeman, but had bought the old Jackson place, which meant I must be doing well for myself because they were asking a pretty penny for it. On top of that, somebody else said I was teaching at the college, but no one believed the college would ever allow that.

My high school baseball coach came into the bank. Twenty-five years ago we placed second in the State Tournament. I attended every game as team statistician.

"Hello, Coach," I said.

"Why, Chris Offutt. I thought you died in Vietnam."

"I'm too young."

"How's your mom and dad?"

"They're doing good, Coach."

"Looks to me like you growed some."

"About six inches."

"I've got a videotape of when we won the regional tournament. One old boy frog-jumped right over you. Just put his hands on your head and pole-vaulted. You should come and see it."

"I'd like that," I said.

We grinned at each other, unsure what to say next. He doubled as the driver's education teacher and I wanted to tell him I still drove safely. That sounded like something a moron would say, so I remained silent. In high school I never shut up and the coach seemed puzzled by this change.

The vice president of MSU Personnel, whom I'd met earlier that day, walked into the bank. I was afraid he'd suspect that I was negotiating a house loan before getting the job. An official offer still had to clear his office, and he could put the kibosh on my plans as easily as brushing away a fly. Terrified that he would see me, I walked quickly away, stepped into a narrow hall, and peered around the corner into the main part of the bank. The vice president was thumbing through his checkbook. Beyond him the coach stared after me as if I were a video he was trying to replay.

I hurried to the bathroom and locked myself in a stall. The door opened and someone entered. I climbed onto the toilet so no one could recognize my shoes. I crouched to prevent my head from appearing above the partition. In a small town you see the same faces several times a day. The by-product of such familiarity is secrecy and paranoia, and I was already beginning to fit in.

Eventually I became embarrassed and stepped boldly into the bank. The coast was clear of university mucketymucks and high school teachers. The loan officer led me into a large office, where we talked for twenty minutes. I told her that MSU had already offered me a job. I told her that the salary was double what I actually expected. I told her that I had journalism work coming out of my ears, foreign rights sold in countries as obscure as Tasmania, and movie deals pending left and right. Everything I said seemed to please her and the more pleased she became, the more the lies flowed from my mouth. She gave me some financial forms that I filled out rapidly. Her family had owned the corner drugstore where I read comic books on Saturday. She recalled having sold me Cokes for a nickel. Her brother was fine; our parents were fine; our spouses were fine. She said the loan was fine.

I walked to the corner drugstore to celebrate with a Coke, but the space had been transformed into a pet store that reeked of urine. The Trail Theatre was closed and the post office had been converted into the police station. I had just bought a house without a job, based on crying in the woods. The hills surrounded me like the dome walls of a snow globe that you shake. Everything in my life was turned over and I was waiting for the flurries to settle. Home, I told myself. I've come home.

I drove to a hotel on the interstate where the desk clerk was a friend of my sister's and the waitress was an old high school teacher. Screwed to the wall of my room was a framed print of a barn with a fading mural that said "Chew Mail Pouch." I unpacked and stared at the ceiling. I needed to call my parents, who still lived in the family home ten miles away. If I failed to call, they'd be upset, but if I did call, I'd have to explain my preference for a hotel room over their house.

I dialed the number that I knew by memory all my life. My parents each listened on an extension. I told them that MSU was paying for the hotel room, and before they had a chance to respond I said I'd found a house. My father asked where the house was. I told him it was off 32 going toward Fleming County, and he said too bad it wasn't closer to their house. My mother said it was closer than Montana at least. That's true, my father agreed, and they began talking with each other, a phone habit that was only truly bothersome if you were calling long distance and didn't feel like paying for them to communicate from different floors of the house.

After a few minutes of listening to them discuss a leak in the roof, I told them I was leaving in the morning but I'd be back in a few weeks.

"Give my love to the boys," my mother said.

"And Rita," I said. "Don't forget Rita."

"Rita, too," my mother said.

"And Rita," my father said. "You can't tell from the drip where the leak comes in."

"That's right," my mother said. "It could be anywhere.

"The chimney," my father said, "that metal part at the shingles."

"Flashing," my mother said. "It's called flashing."

I hung up the phone gently so as not to disturb their conversation. I called Rita and the busy signal throbbed in my head. In the past year I'd suffered my most severe bout of homesickness, a gradual descent of misery to the embarrassing trough of crying over a recipe in an Appalachian cookbook. My sobs awakened Rita who joined me in the living room. She had never seen such grief in me, and assumed it could only be the result of a phone call bearing terrible news. In a tender voice she asked who died. I didn't have the heart to tell her I was mourning my own loss, that a part of me had died the day I left the hills. I was like an amputee feeling perpetual pain in my phantom limb.

The Rowan County phone book consisted of seventy pages and I searched unsuccessfully for a house inspector. I read the white pages for an hour repeating the last names like reciting a prayer. I knew the family histories—where they lived and what ridge or hollow they came from. I had dated them and hated them, fought them and sided with them. I knew their parents, brothers and sisters, first and second cousins. Soon enough I'd know their children. The addresses flowed through my mind. I'd walked the dirt and driven the roads and gotten lost a hundred times. The names were the sounds of home, the language of the land.

Buffalo and Bearskin
Big Perry and Little Perry
Hogtown and Hogge Street
Grassy Lick, Clay Lick, Pond Lick, and Pattie's Lick
Rice Loop and Sharkey
Dry Creek and Dry Branch
Hays Branch and Brushy
Rock Fork, Bull Fork, Open Fork
Sugar Loaf
Lower Licking
Morehead

Reading these made me feel like a solitary immigrant who'd found a fellow countryman and could finally talk the native tongue. I slipped the phone book beneath my pillow and went to sleep with the rhythms of home coursing through my head like a freight train.

In June, Rita and I packed a truck in the Rocky Mountains and began a three-day trek to the Appalachian Mountains. We had moved every year for a decade and believed that this was the last stop. I was delirious with the prospect of living in Kentucky. My mother always said a map of the state looked like a typewriter turned sideways, and I repeated this to my sons. Sam looked at me with a puzzled expression and said, "What's a typewriter?"

At ages eight and five, Sam and James were too young to remember past visits, but they had heard me talk of Kentucky all their lives. It was the promised land of milk and honey. There were no bullies in paradise, no burglars, bad guys, or bums. Everyone loved children. The boys could walk barefoot, have pets, go fishing, explore the woods. They were, as Sam said, "totally psyched" to live there.

Twenty years ago I'd left on foot with a backpack and was now returning in a moving truck full of furniture. I also arranged for the transport of a 1968 Malibu—red with a black interior—that I had bought from two men who co-owned it in a Montana trailer park. It had a shifter kit, short pipes, a 327-cubic-inch engine, three moonie hubcaps, and a double-pump carburetor. Like me, the body was beat to pieces, but it could reach a hundred miles per hour in less than eight seconds, the perfect rig for the hills.

The mathematics of time is as arbitrary as it is precise. Depending on how you counted, I'd been gone five years since my last visit; ten years since getting married and living a few months on my home hill; or twenty years since I'd hitchhiked into America. To my neighbors I'd never left, but merely been visiting away for a spell. Until the Haldeman post office had closed, I still received mail there. I had left Kentucky several times forever. Now I was going back for good.

On the third day of travel we reached I-64, the last leg of America's interstate system, built while I was a kid. It was the widest road in the county and we called it "the four-laner," a verbal habit I had to break after leaving the hills and learning that four lanes was not all that big.

We crossed the dark and twisty Licking River into my home county. Early buds dappled the slopes with a gauze of green in the morning mist. Looming above the river was the Pottsdale Escarpment, a geographic formation that marked the eastern edge of the Appalachian Mountains. The escarpment rose from the land like a forbidding wall, a river of earth, a stone hieroglyph. Beyond it lay my past and future.

Rita loved the house, the private bath, the view of the woods. Never before had each boy had his own bedroom. The kitchen was big, the appliances new. We had a guest room, two bathrooms, a large garage, and a balcony overlooking a pond. The finished basement held a separate room that was ideal for writing.

The first night we ate pizza and went to bed early. James stirred in his bed, half asleep. I moved him crossways on the mattress and smoothed the old quilt. It was frayed and falling apart, but he insisted on sleeping with it despite the heat. A year before he asked why we owned such a ratty blanket, and I was embarrassed by the truth—it was all we could afford. Instead I told him it was my blanket as a child. Our family had no actual heirlooms, and this secondhand quilt was all he knew of an imagined past. Kentucky would give him history.

In two months I would turn forty years old. I felt fortunate to have everything I wanted—a family, a career, a house in the woods of home. The world at large called me a Kentuckian, but in the state, I was from Rowan County. Within that realm I was a Haldeman boy, and to the people there I was from the first hill above the school.

During the next few weeks Rita and the boys explored Morehead and visited my parents at the other end of the county. We unpacked slowly. I had never felt so happy, so enthusiastic for life. I intended to grow old here. I would be buried among the trees. Wildflowers would grow on my grave. Until then, I would help young people understand themselves, and provide an example of the potential for life beyond the hills. I had come home to give as much as possible. Eventually I might move into politics. As an insider, I knew more than anyone what the hills needed. Just as important, I knew what we didn't need—no more sympathy, no more mindless federal programs, no more assistance by outsiders.

Morehead State University is a poor school in a poor state. Forty percent of people don't finish high school, a low number compared to the surrounding area. Eastern Kentucky offers no models for success, no paths for ambitious people to follow, no tangible life beyond the county line. Doing well is a betrayal of mountain culture. Gaining money means you have screwed somebody over and going on vacation implies you don't like living here. Most glaringly absent from eastern Kentucky is a sense of pride. I hoped to fix that.

A month after our arrival, Rita's parents visited. They emigrated from Poland in 1946 and have lived in New York ever since. The first time I met them was on my birthday when Rita and I were dating in Manhattan. Her parents joined us at a restaurant. They were nearly seventy and still working twelve-hour days. Arthur was a chief draftsman for an architectural firm in the World Trade Center. Irene counseled terminal cancer patients at Memorial Sloan-Kettering Hospital. Over supper, Arthur mentioned that his brother had the same birthday as mine.

"He must be a great guy," I said.

Everyone stared at their plates. A palpable tension filled the air. I didn't know what had happened until Irene spoke.

"He was," she said. "He was a nice boy. He died in the camps. So sad."

"Yes," I said. "I'm sorry."

Just as rapidly the discomfort faded and the meal progressed with renewed cheer. I cursed myself for having forgotten that both her parents were Holocaust survivors. Everyone else in their family had been murdered by the Nazis. Arthur's brother simply disappeared, leaving Arthur with the wisp of hope that his brother was still living.

Arthur drives German cars. He shops as if he's still in Europe, with stops at the bakery, the deli, the fruit and vegetable stand. He chats with the shopkeepers like they are close friends. He and Irene seldom disagree, but when they do, they speak Polish. They enjoy giving presents. They never laugh.

Mirrors line the walls of their duplex. The bathroom has three mirrors, and one entire wall of the dining room is paneled in reflective glass. I wondered if this lent the illusion of space or reminded Arthur and Irene of their own existence. Their youth was spent in deprivation wearing rags. Now they are always impeccably dressed and groomed, hair combed, nails clipped, necks scented with cologne. I have never seen Arthur without his shirt tucked into freshly pressed pants held in place by a shiny belt. Irene's hair invariably appears beauty shop perfect. Her clothes fit well, are tasteful and stylish.

Arthur and Irene have drawn a line through time—before the war and after the war. For fifty years they lived under the protection of the Statue of Liberty. In Kentucky, they each agreed to tell me their story. I went to town and bought a microcassette recorder. I began to listen.

Arthur Goes to War

I was drafted in 1939. They sent me to the border of Germany and Poland, not far from my house. The war started there in September on my twentieth birthday. The war was over in the first couple of days.

The Luftwaffe just came from nowhere. A lot of noise. The whole countryside was one big perpetuation of light and explosions. We took many casualties. The Germans dug themselves in. We were trapped. They sent me and another guy back through German lines to get help. There were woods, there were fields, there were farmhouses. Very picturesque. It's beautiful.

I was crawling and the Germans were talking rather casually. I had a rifle but I had to get rid of it. I was afraid of making noise. I was crawling all night in the potato fields. I have never seen such a full moon. A beautiful night, like daylight. I crawled and crawled. Every time I touched a dead soldier I felt relief. Every time I touched a soldier who was not dead, I felt bad. My friend chose the wrong direction. I never saw him again.

Headquarters was gone so I joined a new unit. The next day we were attacked. The unit was destroyed and everybody was dead. I went to the city I used to live in and found my father. He was angry because he thought I deserted. No, I said, we lost.

I didn't take off my boots for a week, and when I did I found a piece of shrapnel in my foot three inches long. I sat in a wheelbarrow and my father pushed me. The German army got us. They saw that my leg was hurt, so an injection I got. They said the war is over, you guys better go home. They gave us food. They gave us a ride to a hospital in Kraków. The hospital is impossible. There was no space. I was tagged to be amputated. I dragged myself to the outhouse, and felt a warmth in my leg, very funny feeling, and the pain eased up. Everything just burst open and pus came out, a real mess. I get a stick and drag myself home. I was laid up, and this was still within a month after the war started.

All the Jews had to report to the government, otherwise

you couldn't get any food. You couldn't buy food in the store anyhow without an ID card. And on the ID card, naturally, it said, boom, Jew. Shortly after the ID cards came out, all the Jews have to wear visible signs on their clothes. In Kraków it was a blue band, white Star of David, which I wore very proudly. But then it was inconvenient.

After they forbid Jews from travel, they took an old part of Kraków, threw a wall around it, collected all the Jews and brought them there. They created a ghetto. The conditions were just appalling. No plumbing. No heat. No food. People were sick. People died of malnutrition, typhoid, dysentery. They were bringing in every day Jews from the surrounding cities. The way they put cattle into a corral, they corralled men. It was inhuman.

The Germans created a Jewish Police with complete power over everybody. Whatever had to be done was done through them. They were willing to do the dirty work for the Germans. The Jewish Police pushed people into the arms of the German SS guards. You're told by this guy, the same religion, same nationality, same language, you're told to go. This is deplorable, it's indescribable. A nightmare. You can't defy these guys who are wearing batons, and they don't wait for you to make a decision. They hit you with that stick.

My mother came home to us one day and said, the police have your father and I go to him. You are big boys; you're on your own. She told me to take care of my brother. She never came back. I never saw my mother and father again.

Irene Goes to the Ghetto

In ghetto I was seventeen. I know Arthur already ten years. Everybody has to work someplace, slave labor. They give me a job with a family and I'm supposed to be their cook and iron their shirts and all this. I think that's the end of my life because I don't know how to do these things. So lucky me, there was a main maid who was Polish, but nice. Very unusual. She showed me how to iron the shirt and what kind of food they liked and how to prepare it.

My mother was in the line to live or die. I had my father's Iron Cross. It was the highest authority medal that existed in Germany. He received it in World War I. He was a colonel in the Austrian army and he saved many German lives. I showed the Iron Cross to the person picking who would live, so she let my mother go. Three months later they choose lives again. But this time it is SS man. He was mad that I showed the Iron Cross. He took the Iron Cross and shot my mother in front of me. My mother was killed before my eyes. On the street. The SS. By the pistol.

Then they sent me to an apartment that the Germans took over from the Jews. He came with his family, the name of Jore. He was the director of a construction company for the army. When I came in first time, I saw there was a piano, and I played pretty well yet. I remembered the Chopin waltz, and I played and he came and said, oh, you're playing piano. They started to ask me questions and give me a lot of bread and tea, just because of one piece on the piano. I never played it again. Chopin saved my life.

Nine-Mile at the Video Store

There is a short stretch of highway between I-64 and Morehead, where a new Wal-Mart has slowly gnawed the town to bits. Morehead storefronts hold nothing but tape on the window cracks. A harebrained remedy to the loss of business was realigning Main Street so that it slithered like a snake. A triangular-shaped wedge of concrete protruded from the corner of every other block. These giant slices of cement pizza ran six blocks, forcing cars to weave a zigzag pattern. People said the cops should use Main Street as a means of testing drunk drivers—anyone who could drive it was sober.

This beautification project transformed Morehead into an obstacle one must circumvent on the way to the mall. You can take the bypass through town, but the lack of traffic lights and turning lanes makes it slow as grandmaw. What we really need is a bypass for the bypass.

The video store at the mall has replaced the general store as the place to visit with neighbors. Aside from church, it is the only place where families see each other. People from two counties away come to Morehead for Wal-Mart, but only locals rent videos. Foreign movies are not available in Rowan County, unless you count *Road Warrior.* Documentary films are confined to hunting, fishing, and National Geographic. Action movies occupy the most shelf space, then thrillers, westerns, and comedies. Porn movies are kept in a back room, but the town is too small for anyone to risk being seen going in or coming out.

While walking the store's aisles I study people near my age, narrowing their features to seek the ghost of who they once were. Anyone on either side of forty receives my wave. The other day I nodded to a man whose posture I recalled. We called him Nine-Mile because he could run fast. He hit puberty in fifth grade and began sleeping in class until high school, where he became a star athlete. Nine-Mile played three sports, drove a Dodge Charger, and dated the prettiest girl from the other end of the county. I admired him tremendously but he ignored me.

These facts entered my mind like an exploding time capsule. His voice was casual, as if we'd seen each other last week instead of two decades ago.

"If it ain't Chris Offutt," he said. "I heard you was in. You doing all right?"

From a great distance, I heard my voice tell him I was picking up videos for the kids. He pointed out his seven children and smiled with pride. Their ages spanned twenty years. One of his young boys ran to him, clutching an empty movie box.

"Put that back, honey," Nine-Mile said. "You've seen that before."

"I have?"

"Yes siree, you have. That movie's the best thing since eggs, but run and get you a new one."

The boy hurried to the shelf. Nine-Mile turned to me and spoke.

"His memory's about as long as his pecker."

"I have the same problem."

He laughed and I gestured to the videotape under his arm.

"What movie you getting?" I said.

"I'm bringing back *Deliverance.* You seen it?"

"Yeah. The music in it's good."

"I didn't like it one bit."

I stepped closer, eager to hear his opinions. I despise the movie's stereotypical depiction of rural people. Nine-Mile's disdain was a pleasant surprise.

"How come you not to like it?" I said.

"At the end when that old boy gets shot with a crossbow,

the arrow sticks out of his chest. As close as he was, it'd go right through him."

"I never thought about it," I said.

"Oh, yeah. I'm a bow-hunter. When I see something in a movie that's supposed to be real but ain't, I'm done with it."

"What about the way those country people were?"

"A pretty rough bunch, if you ask me. I'd not fool with them. They're from so far back in the hills they went toward town to hunt."

I laughed as he scanned the aisles for his kids.

"You still writing books?" he said.

"Yes."

"Good trade. It's nice to see a Haldeman boy make something of hisself."

"I just worked hard and got lucky is all."

"Do you print them up yourself?"

"No, there's a company in New York that takes care of that for me."

"I see," he said. "You subcontract it out."

"Something like that."

"How long's it take to write a book, Chris? About a month?"

"Longer for me. What makes you think a month?"

"That's when they change the paperbacks at Wal-Mart."

The conversation stopped, but I knew he wanted to talk. We both stood awkwardly. I studied his large hands, once so adept with a football and basketball, now gnarled and battered like old tools. He was missing two fingers.

"What are you doing these days?" I said.

"I'm a logger and a tobacco farmer. Guess I'm what you'd call an endangered species. I'm getting out of farming. No money."

"What'll you go into next?"

"I don't know. I ain't thought that far ahead."

A child began to cry and Nine-Mile smiled apologetically and hurried away. Like many generations before him, he was engaged in the only industry offered by the land where he was born. Stores give credit until the tobacco harvest and every fall the new clothes on schoolkids will tell you how the prices are running at the burley auction. Nine-Mile lived on land his family had always owned and made a living from.

He retrieved a five-year-old girl and held her against his chest. Nine-Mile's face softened to the boy I remembered, and it occurred to me that I should have lived in an earlier time. I'd still have the same personality, the same ancient soul. Born in the eighteenth century, I'd lament having missed the wonders of the seventeenth. If I were living in the Renaissance, I'd probably feel nostalgic for the Middle Ages. Continuing this way would make me a Cro-Magnon in a cave envying his brethren who still lived in the trees.

I left the video store with several movies for the kids. The afternoon sun leaned into the hills across the parking lot, surrounded by chain stores that manacled the land. Across the vast sea of black tar stood Wal-Mart. People were excited when Wal-Mart first arrived until the low prices killed local stores. Now there is nowhere else to shop. It cares as little for its customers as the old company store in my hometown did. The only difference is that scrip is legal in the form of a charge card. If Wal-Mart doesn't carry an item, you are compelled to do without. People accept this with typical mountain resignation, putting a melancholy forward spin on it with a new slogan: Everything's at Wal-Mart. Technically that's true, because if something isn't there, it does not exist here.

Behind Wal-Mart like a ramparts to the hills is the first planned development in Rowan County. The neighborhood was such a success that the Church of God closed its doors in town and built a new one behind the mall. It is now known as the Wal-Mart Church of God.

One is tempted to say that Wal-Mart killed what was once a thriving town. One could just as well blame the interstate. The real culprit is the end of the rail industry. This was preceded by the decline of the riverboat era, the invention of the horseless buggy, the westward expansion, the discovery of the Cumberland Gap, the European invasion, the Puritan pioneers and subsequent waves of immigration, the voyages of Columbus, the Viking explorers, the landbridge walkers, the death of the dinosaurs, and the great breaking apart of the continents.

All of this ruined Morehead in twenty years.

Arthur Meets Irene

I knew Irene when she was ten years old. We used to go for vacations together. She was just a girl. I was a boy. I found Irene after they shot her mother. She wasn't even crying, she was just laying there. There were at least eight, nine people in the room. And that room was ten by twelve feet. The beds were separated by a curtain for some kind of privacy. The smell was magnificent. Electricity was on and off. I spent the first night with my wife in this Devil's kitchen. What do you say to somebody who's lost everything? She couldn't save her mother; she was just devastated. What do you say to her? Let's make the best of it? I said nothing. She just laid there in my arms. The next day I told her, you're gonna be with me as long as we can.

Irene Finds Freedom

In camp, if it was not going the way I like, I never despair. I disconnect my thoughts. I don't think about the tragic things. I think of something else which is more pleasant or nice for me. When I disconnect I think that just surviving is the most important and then forget about it. I have terrible fear. I suffered the most from fear. I was scared of everything around me, but when I disconnect, it's like not me. Somebody else.

We eat potato soup, the skins. That saved us because that's the most healthy part, but they didn't know it. Once a week a piece of bread. All the women stopped menstruating.

As a girl I wasn't very happy. My sister was dead and my

father was dying. So my mother did everything for me. She picked my clothes. She pick my friends. She pick what I do, where I go, what I eat. In camp she picks nothing. For the first time, I have freedom.

Beginning the Book

The odd thing about this book is I never set out to write it. The audiotapes were intended for the kids and the rest came from my journals. When I hit on the idea of bringing these disparate narratives together, I called Arthur for permission to use the tapes. There was a long silence on the phone, until he said, "To write this book, Sonny, is like telling the lions not to eat the antelope."

Now I call him once a week to double-check facts and details. Spelling Polish proper nouns is confounding, and my attempts at syllabic representation produce gobbledygook. Our conversations trigger his memory and I take notes as we talk. Soon, I begin transcribing all that he says.

Arthur's life is hard now. His neighborhood in Queens has changed and no one will shovel snow from his walk.

His car inexplicably became filled with ice, his basement with water. Irene has Parkinson's disease and requires a great deal of care. He is a little depressed. I ask if he's reading, and he says yes, a book on the Spanish Inquisition.

He is not angry at the German army because he was a soldier and understands the mentality of serving one's country. He feels most betrayed by his fellow Poles, especially members of the Jewish Police.

As the conversation begins to wane, his voice takes on a tone of concern.

"I don't want to ask, Sonny. But something is nagging at me a little."

"It's all right, Arthur. Ask me anything."

"What bothers me is this. How will you link the two stories. The war and Kentucky. What joins them?"

"I don't know, Arthur. I'm worried about that myself."

"You figure it out, Sonny. I have faith. Maybe something subliminal."

"The ending," I say. "Maybe the ending will pull it all together."

"All endings are the same, Sonny. You die. The scene in the *Titanic* movie was the closest I've ever seen to the camps—one against the other. The good people don't survive. You have to push a little to get into the lifeboat. There was one scene of two old people watching it all, then they went to their bed and lay down and waited to die. At that point, I could not look. It was my attitude exactly. But I lived. I always lived. That was the problem. I lived."

I hang up the phone, impressed by the prescience of his concern. At first I thought the notion of home would bind the narratives—my constant desire to return, his utter commitment to never go back. My original plan was for us to visit Poland together, but he refused. I suggested a trip to Israel, and again he refused. Traveling to the Holocaust Museum in Washington, D.C., was also dismissed.

I considered making a trip to Poland alone, visiting Kraków, finding cemeteries, standing in the very room where Arthur was born. This seemed as depressing a prospect as reading about the Inquisition and I quickly abandoned the plan. In fact, all my ideas seemed pathetic. I finally decided that the ending would be whatever happened during my life while writing the book.

The Library and Mrs. Jayne

Mrs. Jayne lived all her life in Morehead, and if she had not always been content, she'd made her peace long ago. Occasionally she'd tell a story about going to Lexington with her girlfriends, referring to the trip as "a bunch of country women on the loose." Mrs. Jayne was my first-grade teacher.

She loved the boys and girls of Haldeman, and we loved her back in the fierce way of children who express elemental emotion with every cell in their bodies. Her house held photographs of people she'd taught, their spouses, their babies, their grandchildren. She was a widow with no kids of her own, and her former students served as family. Each year I sent Mrs. Jayne a Christmas card. I visited when I went home and several years ago I'd introduced her to Rita. All my grandparents were dead. I wanted Sam and James to know Mrs. Jayne.

I drove to her house, thinking of the car I owned in college, a red Maverick that leaked Bondo at the seams. To save money I parked in Mrs. Jayne's driveway, which was a block from campus. She said she liked seeing the car and knowing one of her first graders had made it to college.

Now Mrs. Jayne was in her eighties. She never locked her door and was hard of hearing. To visit, you walked into her breezeway and began calling yoo-hoo to avoid startling her. Today she didn't answer and I found her asleep in an easy chair. I gazed around the living room at all the photographs, including one of my sons propped on the mantel. When I was a kid her house was the most proper I'd ever been inside, containing stiff furniture that was uncomfortable to sit on. Later I understood that she lived among lovely antiques that she kept neat and clean, despite using them daily. Now I recognized that everything was a little messy—a pillow on the floor, a rumpled afghan, a water stain on an end table. I tiptoed out. The kids were disappointed and I told them we'd visit the Rowan County Public Library.

I was the first kid to step inside the library when it

opened in 1967. The head librarian was Frankie Calvert, related by marriage to Mrs. Jayne. One woman taught me to read and the other placed books in my hands each week. I loved them as a child and my devotion had never faltered.

Due to the library's limited holdings, you could only check out four books at a time per library card. Since I read at least one book a day, and more during school vacations and weekends, I circumvented the rules by getting library cards for all my siblings, two of whom were not yet in school, as well as a card in the name of the family dog. My mother went to town every Saturday for groceries. She dropped me at the library where I borrowed twenty books, stacked them in a grocery bag, and waited for her to retrieve me. By age ten I knew the Dewey Decimal System inside out.

Now I entered the library with great enthusiasm. A woman from Haldeman was working there and I asked about her family. She hadn't changed much and I wondered if she thought the same of me. Frankie came out of her office and we hugged briefly, a part of me disappointed that she was not thirty years younger. Frankie possessed a lilting accent native to the hills that is impossible to duplicate in writing. She looked at my sons and said, "They sure are good-looking boys." She pronounced "boys" with two syllables, as if it were spelled "bo-eeze." Another mountain trait is repetition and she said it again, carrying me into the past and hearing her tell my mother the same about me.

Frankie showed Sam to the children's section where he began browsing with the experience of a seasoned library kid. James shyly took her hand as she led him to a special spot. She perched on the edge of a tiny chair, leaned forward with a book in her hands, and read aloud to him. James stared at her face, enraptured by her attention. I recalled listening to her in the same way at his age. When Frankie read to me, she'd been younger than I was now. I felt as if time had altered from a linear progression to one of overlapping concentric rings. I had never left Morehead, but been bumped ahead, with remnants of memory all around me.

I wandered the library, stunned to realize that no one else was there on a Saturday afternoon. During college I had put on magic shows for children here, using tricks I'd made from how-to books. The illusions were simple—cut and restored rope, the production of scarves from a tube, an empty bag that contained eggs. The magic books were gone, hopefully to a child busy at home folding cardboard into secret gimmicks. Inside a battered book, I discovered a check-out card. The signature was mine, dated 1968.

Holding a book that had passed through my hands so

long ago gave me a sudden chill that drifted into bliss. The protagonist's name was Eddie. He liked to write notes and post them in his house. I copied his behavior, taping my words to various places in our home. I remembered the name of Eddie's dog, his best friend, and his enemy. In books, I found kids who shared my interest and adults who appreciated me.

I pulled the oldest books from the shelf and examined each card. Several bore my name from thirty years before, and I made a pile of these books for Sam, enthralled that he would read them at the same age as I had. The presence of my signature indicated that no new card had ever been required. Don't be sad, I told myself. That's why you came home—to help fix problems like this.

We checked out the books and walked into the heat of summer. The hills were dulled by the humidity that hung in the air like old breath. Sam was disappointed in the library. He had carefully looked over the books and found nothing contemporary, nothing similar to what he'd been reading for the past year. I gave him the Eddie books.

We returned to visit Mrs. Jayne who yoo-hooed back, fully awake now. I hugged her and she felt fragile as papyrus. She'd lost weight and her clothes didn't fit, reminding me that she'd always taken great care of her appearance. She insisted on sitting in the backyard to receive summer guests. The boys adored her as if they'd known her all their lives. She sent me inside to pour glasses of "co-cola" for everyone. The kitchen smelled terrible. Dirty dishes filled the sink. The garbage had not been emptied in a long time.

I scrubbed some glasses, poured the drinks, and carried them outside. Mrs. Jayne was talking to the boys with such care that I suddenly understood why children were drawn to her. She would never judge a child, never criticize, never tamper with innocence. She behaved as if every child was her particular favorite. She still treated me that way and I still basked in her attention.

I motioned Rita inside and showed her the state of the house. She said, "I'll clean the bathroom, you do the kitchen." We found supplies and worked for an hour. I was tidying the living room when Sam and James entered the house with fearful expressions. I asked what was the matter and Sam spoke, taking the lead as oldest, the way I always had as a child.

"Something's wrong with Mrs. Jayne."

"She might be dead," James said.

Tears flowed over his cheeks as he rushed to me and hugged my waist. I called for Rita, who sat with James on the couch while I went to the backyard. Mrs. Jayne sat in her chair asleep. I took the empty glasses inside and made the boys laugh with the truth of Mrs. Jayne. We walked to the car, but I didn't like leaving her in the yard in case the weather shifted or the sunlight burned her pale skin. I went back through the breezeway to help her in the house. Her eyes fluttered open.

"Well, Chris," she said. "What a wonderful surprise. Sit down and let's have a visit."

"Okay."

"When are you bringing those boys of yours for me to meet?"

"Let's go inside, Mrs. Jayne."

"We'll have us some co-cola."

"I can't stay too long."

"You have a busy life now, Chris. There's one thing I want you to know. I'm just so proud of you for teaching at Morehead. I want you to park in my driveway. It'll be easy for you to walk to work. I like seeing a man's car in the driveway."

"Okay, Mrs. Jayne."

She eased into her chair, reminding me of a feather pillow slowly settling into comfort. Within a few minutes she was asleep again. On my way out I stopped in the breezeway. Leaning against the wall were alphabet posters that had hung in my first-grade classroom, and I remembered writing words that began with each letter. I drove home, understanding that naively and perhaps foolishly, I wanted life in Rowan County to be the same as thirty years ago. I wanted Frankie to give me books and Mrs. Jayne to be healthy.

Later, Sam said he didn't like the Eddie books because they were too much like the old days. He wanted to read about the world of today.

Arthur Works at a Labor Camp

In labor camp I am helper to a master surveyor, running around with that stick, doing land surveying for the airport facilities. I had a job, and was able to wash myself every day. This is the best time of my war years. It was peaceful. They didn't mistreat us. It was slave labor.

My wife worked in the kitchen and in the evening I was able to visit her. We worked only about ten hours a day. We had Sunday off and we took old clothing and tied them into little pieces for socks. I could not sleep with her but I was able to take care of her. She smuggled potatoes to me and I traded on the black market. I buy panties for her, some soap.

I was going with my boss by the hospital in the ghetto. There was a big driveway that was shut by a wooden gate.

My boss asked me what's that, and I said that used to be the hospital. He said, open the gate. I want to see what's in that. So we opened the gate and inside is full of corpses, people shot. They were just laying maybe ten high. The courtyard was filled with corpses, children mostly. Piled up like lumber. Just thrown in the garbage. It was the first time I saw corpses piled up that way. The first time.

They sent my brother to another camp and I did not see him again. I never saw him ever. I don't know where he is buried. He was sixteen.

I was working in the rain and lo and behold, I catch pneumonia. My boss likes me. He drove me to the hospital in camp where my wife is. And now I am happy. I have a clean bed. Out my window is the place where they bring the people every day and shoot them. Every day. Most are people who are caught in the resistance. When the sun came up, two guys came on motorcycles and then the trucks. Everybody off the truck, undress, line up in front of the pit, shoot them, fall in the pit. Sometimes they shoot into the pit if somebody was moving. Then they poured in gasoline and burned it. That thing was like a hell smoking, continuously smoking, day in, day out. They put in railroad ties because it is very difficult to burn bodies. The air has to circulate, otherwise they don't burn. So the bodies from yesterday are still smoldering. The pit is smoking all the time. Fifty yards from my window. I could see faces. I could see everything. That was my morning.

So I send out the good news that I am in the camp. An old man was dying, so I put on his uniform, and sneaked out to find my wife. She cut her own hair and it looks good. She has a little more hair than other women. Just a little more, but it makes all the difference. She starved herself and bought a comb. She took her uniform, which was shit, you know, and she tied it and made it fit her. It didn't look like a piece of something hung on her. It looked good. She was very beautiful, my wife.

She took me to her barracks. They had bunks stacked on top of each other and they run from one end of the camp to the other. There were curtains drawn between each of those. You crawled in from the front and you drew the curtains. They were, I would say, two hundred feet long. Thousands of people. They were shitting and pissing and vomiting and screwing and eating and washing, all in the same area. If a man or woman was able to organize something to eat, they cook it right there. It looked like some kind of pure hell.

My wife remained untouched. She was like Mr. Magoo on the cartoon. All the chaos surrounding him and he is untouched. She has a certain naïveté in her left. She is Mrs. Magoo still. There is no malice in her. She was witnessing rape and murder by the day. My wife, when she was young, she was built like a statue. Very distinguished. She had nice features and she was courageous.

We have one foot of privacy, and I spent the second night with my wife there. I was just holding her. I couldn't protect her from this. She was an angel in hell. That was the last time I saw my wife till after the war. Three years.

Irene Is Saved in Plaszow

The first camp was the worst, Plaszow. It was very scary. Every week somebody beaten up, somebody killed. It was a lot of punishing, a lot of fear. From every corner, you look the dead in the eye. The worst part was the loneliness, the unexpected, the fear. I'm a coward.

Goeth was the camp leader, chairman, or whatever you call it. He was shooting people weekly. He needed that blood. He had to have food for his soul. Every day was some explosion. Goeth was a devil. Goeth came to choose the people for death. He just pulled this one, this one, this one. There was no reason, no special reason why. You should not look at his eyes. When you look at his eyes, he was furious. Right away he was shooting. A real devil. If you saw *Schindler's List,* you know who that was. He was the one with the young girl he was beating up.

Goeth came to the factory where I worked. The manager from before the war, Nasia, she looked at me and said you go down in the hole to hide. That was all. I went and she put the paper over the hole. I was in the dark listening and hearing Goeth say, this one, this one, this one. All to die. When he left, she took me out of there. I was lucky.

She died in New York, Nasia Geitshals. I was in her funeral. Beth-Moses Cemetery on Long Island. Where I will go one day. With Arthur. We go.

No Heroes

My editor inquires if Arthur is excited that I am writing a book about him. I don't know, I say. I get off the phone and call Arthur and tell him my editor wants to know how he feels about the book. He says that he wears a nightshirt to sleep in. It is not so long, the nightshirt, and sometimes he has to pull it down to cover his uh-ohs. The book makes him feel like the nightshirt is rolled up. I tell him that is the nature of art. I ask him if he wants me to roll his shirt back down. It's not too late.

"No," he says, "but one thing."

"What?"

"No heroes."

"Why not?"

"Heroes are not human."

"What about Moses?"

"He's no hero! He's all confused. God was always mad at him. God tried to kill him three times. He's no hero. He didn't want to go up that mountain. God had to talk him into it. If God would talk to me, I would run to do it. If that happened to you, Sonny, what would you do?"

"It would terrify me. I'd think I was crazy."

"I'd be the happiest man in the world. God bothers to talk to me—to *me!* I'd know what life was for. What is the reason to live—kids, build the Empire State Building, make a painting, eat? Then a meteor hits the earth and we are gone. Humans are nothing. If God talked to me, I could die in peace."

We say good-bye and hang up. Kentucky is a long state composed of two sections—the hills and the blacktop. All our heroes come from the blacktop. The Appalachian region claims no heroes, and the inhabitants have learned to live without the hope of one. During college I walked the streets of Morehead with a button pinned to my jacket that read "No Heroes." I wore it proudly, eager for everyone to see my late-seventies political stance. I read Rimbaud, listened to the Clash, and wore sleeveless cowboy shirts. I left to change the world, but as much as I tried, I was no hero, either.

First Day of School

As a kid I never liked school, I was just good at it. Teachers helped me at every stage—Mrs. Jayne in first grade, Mrs. Hardin in fifth grade, Mr. Ellington in seventh. Mrs. Walke and Mrs. Slone looked after me in high school. During college I entered the province of men—Marc Glasser, Bill Layne, Joe Sartor. My goal as a teacher was to emulate the best ones. I hoped every student would eventually remember me as the teacher who'd made a difference, the one who took an interest, listened, and cared.

In the meantime, I couldn't decide what to wear to the first day of class. Blue jeans and boots, of course, and a short-sleeve shirt because the humidity was like breathing through a wet wasp nest. I finally settled on my most conservative shirt—blue paisley with red trim. It was the kind of shirt I'd never have worn as a student because people might think I was a sissy. In my new role I wanted to set an example that was contrary to mountain dress for men.

I drove the Malibu proudly, enjoying the attention its rumbling engine commanded as I deliberately cruised the length of campus, giving a little extra gas in front of the administration building. Many people believe that the education problems in eastern Kentucky are due to the quality of instruction at Morehead State University. Over the years, MSU went from being a beacon in the wilderness to a dim light shining primarily on itself. The mission statement of serving the region is impossible to meet as long as the university kowtows to coal companies for financial contributions.

The students were my people, from my hills, at my school but I was nervous as a long-tailed cat in a room full of rocking chairs. I parked at Mrs. Jayne's house and gathered breath deep into my lungs. I can do this, I said to myself.

I walked briskly to campus, sweating through my shirt, stumbling twice over minuscule imperfections in the pavement. My assigned office was in a small house that had been a private medical office. Instead of framed diplomas on the wall, I hung a map of eastern Kentucky counties. I opened my notes and reviewed my lecture to each of the four writing classes: Creative Nonfiction, Advanced Undergraduate Fiction, Graduate Fiction Writing, and Intro to Creative Writing. I had taught these courses elsewhere, but it was my first experience teaching four classes in one day.

Just before nine o'clock, I left my office and drank coffee from a Styrofoam cup, watching students stroll to class. The majority were quiet and clean-cut and I wondered what became of the contemporary version of myself—long hair, ragged clothes—and how I would recognize the ones I came to help. Hip-hop music spilled from low-rider pick-ups driven by boys with their hats on backward. Many cars had tinted windows embellished with gothic script. "Only God can judge me," read one, a line from a Tupac Shakur song, the perfect phrase to embody hostile rebellion in the Bible Belt. Kentucky has 120 counties, more than any other state, and license plates display the driver's home county. Those cars playing the loudest were from deepest in the hills, and I knew that some of the drivers had never seen a black person except on television.

I dumped my coffee and headed for class, entering the stream of people. I stopped in front of the English building and reminded myself that I was a teacher now, not a student. The bushes rattled behind me. "Hey, Chris," someone said. Out stepped Harley, a boy I'd grown up with in Haldeman, now in his late thirties. His breath smelled of whiskey. I'd not seen him in over a decade.

"Damn, Harley, you like to scared me to death."

"The law went by a minute ago is all."

"Are they hunting you?"

"I forgot if they are or not. I just always hide."

"Well," I said. "They ain't around right now."

"I got half a joint in my pocket if you want to come up in the woods and burn one with me."

"I can't, Harley. I start a new job today."

"They say you're a schoolteacher now."

"I just fell into it."

"They're hard up, my opinion."

"You working?"

"Hell no," he said. "I get the crazy check."

"You ain't crazy, Harley."

"I know it, but the State don't. And don't you go telling them nothing, either."

"You'd best get up in them woods," I said. "Come on, we'll cut through the building."

"Son, we ain't allowed in the college."

"I am, Harley."

I led him into the English building, through a hall thronged with students to the rear exit. He put his head down as if in custody, walking in a slow way to make sure he didn't make a mistake. We went outside and he pointed to the tree line at the top of the hill.

"That's my spot," he said. "You come up later and we'll burn one. I got beer up there, too."

"What are you doing in town this early?"

"College girls, Chris, college girls. They are good to look at in the sun."

"Do you ever talk to them?"

"No. They'd not talk to me. They're too stuck up."

"Maybe you are."

"You shit and fall back in it, Chris. If I'm stuck up, what are you?"

"I'm just a Haldeman boy, same as you."

"That's all I'll ever be, but you're a schoolteacher. By God, they ain't no better thing to be unless it's a doctor, and then you got to dig around in folks' guts all day. What are you teaching anyhow?"

"You know, writing and stuff."

"They say your books are good, Chris. I've read at them without much luck."

"Watch the law, Harley."

"I don't need to," he said. "I got you watching out for me like old times."

He patted his pocket containing the half joint, wiggled his eyebrows, and trudged up the hill. After a few steps he turned back.

"Hey, Chris," he said. "How do you teach writing?"

"That's a good question, Harley. What do you think?"

"Well, if it was me, I'd say to just let them write what was on their mind."

"That's what I'll tell them."

"You sure you can't slip up here for a minute?"

"Thanks, but no."

I watched him climb the hill. Like most people from Haldeman, Harley made it through eighth grade but not high school. He left the sidewalk for the woods and I saw flashes of his shirt moving through the trees as he headed for his spot, the highest point overlooking campus. I knew that he would get stoned, drink a beer, and take a nap. He would awaken thirsty, his head cloudy. He'd smoke a cigarette and check his pockets for money, hoping for enough to buy a bottle of Ale-8 and a Slim Jim at a gas station. Then he'd walk the road until someone picked him up and drove him somewhere. I knew all this because I'd once lived the same way.

A particular quirk of mountain people is to go home as often as possible. Appalachian workers in Ohio factories commonly drive all night after Friday's shift to reach the hills by Saturday morning. This trait has given rise to a joke about hillbillies being chained in Heaven to prevent them going home on the weekends. College students were no exception, and Morehead is known as a "suitcase school," meaning that the vast majority of students went home on Friday.

I walked into my first class late. The students sat in rigid rows of school desks. I announced the name of the class and asked if everyone was in the right room. No one spoke or nodded. I told them to call me by my first name. A few blinked in surprise. At MSU, most professors insist upon being called "Doctor." I gave each student a copy of my course description, read it aloud, and asked for questions. There were none. A long silence ensued during which I looked out the window at maintenance workers busily primping the president's home. When I returned my attention to the students, everyone looked at me, then away. I dismissed class. They left swiftly without a word.

I walked downstairs and sat in the dimly lit theater where the plays I wrote as a student had been produced. The first one was a futuristic retelling of *Oedipus Rex* with a punk rock soundtrack. All the actors wore sunglasses. To gain entry to a gang, Eddie slept with a hooker who turned out to be his mother, and set fire to a wino who was later revealed as his father. Instead of blinding himself at the climax, Eddie removed his sunglasses. This last part I considered a stroke of genius. The music included "The Blank Generation" by Richard Hell, who was not only a Kentuckian but had been born in the same hospital as me. For a few years we had lived half a mile apart in Lexington. After graduation my plan was to leave Kentucky forever. Now I was back at MSU and Richard Hell was fifty years old.

I checked the time and went upstairs to teach another class in much the same fashion as the first. Afterward I walked to the old courthouse and ate a sack lunch. A torpor settled over me like a quilt of sand. It was as though I were inhabiting the past and the future simultaneously, encased in a swaddling that forbade access to the present. I couldn't be a teacher until shedding the memory of being a student.

My graduate fiction writing class met in the same room where I'd been interviewed, with comfortable chairs surrounding tables pushed together. The students included a transfer student from China with extremely limited skills in English. Another was a nontraditional undergraduate who was older than me and tried incessantly to establish common points of reference through geography, event, and people's last names. Another man wanted to tell me what he found objectionable with my books. One young man admitted that he was trying to raise his GPA by taking an easy course. Two women were high school teachers who would get a pay raise after completing the class. We talked briefly about the kind of writing we were interested in pursuing, a gamut that included horror, science fiction, romance, and "*Little House on the Prairie* type books." After class the nontraditional student lingered.

"Ever hear of Andrew Offutt?" he said.

"Yes."

"Is he kin?"

"He's my father."

"I heard he was at a party with some guy with only one

arm. Your daddy yelled out he was going tear that guy's other arm off."

I nodded and the guy left.

I'd become accustomed to Andy Offutt stories all my life. Everyone in the county told them. In fact, my father told this same story often, each time with a rising pride that I never fully comprehended. The one-armed guy had been an MSU administrator, now retired.

The late-afternoon class was Intro to Creative Writing, filled with sophomores and juniors. One student set the tone by claiming that expecting him to turn in assignments interfered with his artistic freedom. He then stomped out, slamming the door. Everyone waited for my reaction.

"Well," I said, "I think we just found a real writer. He knows as well as I do that it's impossible to teach writing. I can help you all learn to revise, but you have to write your own first draft. Any questions?"

A young man slouching in the back row raised his hand and spoke. "You care what we write about?"

"Nope. No rules."

"Good, I don't like rules."

"Me, neither," I said. "And neither did the guy who left."

People laughed and I told them about painting the curbs in front of the very building we were in. A young woman named Sandra said she understood "no rules," but she didn't always know what to write about.

"That's a good question," I said. "This morning a friend of mine suggested that I tell you all to write whatever's on your mind."

I told them about Harley and their attention became downright perky when I mentioned that he had some dope.

"Write what you care about," I said. "Write what hurts you. If there's someone whose approval you want, write about that person."

"What if that's all the same person?"

"Then you're lucky," I said. "You have a lifetime's worth of material."

I ended class shortly after that. The student from the back row ducked back into the room. He wore a flannel shirt over a gangsta-rap T-shirt. His body was marked by tattoos and piercings. Portable stereo headphones dangled around his neck. I asked his name.

"Eugene from Martin County."

I shook his hand and he frowned.

"What's wrong?" I said.

"No teacher ever did that before."

"I'll have to speak to them about that."

"Do you like to read?" he said.

"Sure do," I said. "You?"

"Yes and no. Not what they make you read, but what I like."

"I know what you mean. What do you like to read?"

"Short stories."

"Me, too. Is there any writer you like?"

"I've read James Still, Gurney Norman, and Chris Holbrook."

"Good. You started with the Kentucky writers and now you can expand from there. Why don't you let me bring you a couple of books next class?"

"Buddy, you got a deal."

He nodded and left. I realized that if I were nineteen today, I'd be tattooed like a comic book, with more metal hanging off me than a tackle box. Any play I wrote would have a hip-hop score. I watched Eugene leave, feeling as if I'd found the student I came home to teach.

Sam and James Learn About the Holocaust

Sam is reading *Maus,* a comic book about the Holocaust that depicts Jews as mice and Nazis as cats. Rita worries about the effect on Sam because she learned of her parents' experience at age twelve by watching a film that featured footage from the camps. Until then, she had no idea what her parents had endured.

I think reading *Maus* is a good way for Sam to understand history. Later I'll explain that his grandparents were mice. Every couple of pages Sam asks a question. I decide to sit across the room and transcribe our conversation in the same manner as when talking to Arthur on the phone.

"How do you know you're a Jew?" Sam says.

"Because your mom and dad are Jews."

"Know what I'd do? I'd tell people I'm not a Jew."

"Some people did that."

"I'd leave."

"Some did that, too."

"What's a dictator?" Sam said.

"A boss with an army who makes people do what he wants."

"That's stupid."

"Why?" I said.

"Because you couldn't say he was a bad boss, right?"

"That's one of the problems all right."

"Did all the Germans hate the Jews or did they just do what Hitler said?"

"A little of both."

"Why didn't they kill him?"

"Who?"

"This guy in here, the little mouse guy. They knew he was a Jew and it was World War II. So why didn't they kill him? I mean, these people had the power to kill him and they hated him. So why not?"

I shrug and he goes back to reading. His grandfather has pondered the same question every day for fifty years. Arthur craves a reason for his survival. Irene admits the truth more readily than her husband. She says survival was random and she was lucky, but Arthur doesn't want to believe it is that simple.

Sam goes into the other room and James sits in the same

chair—my chair—and opens *Maus.* He cannot read but he studies the pictures very carefully. He is five years old and wants to be an artist when he grows up.

"Why is this comic book in black and white?" he says.

"Why do you think?"

"Because it was made before color."

After a few minutes, James brings the book to me. He points to a scene of mouse prisoners and cat captors. One prisoner has been promoted to the boss of other prisoners, what Arthur called the Jewish Police. He is drawn with the face of a pig.

"Is this guy a pig?" James asks.

I tell him yes and he wants to know why. I wonder how to explain the cultural metaphor of a pig as a cop. I tell James the guy's a pig because the cat and mouse faces were already used. That satisfies him and he returns to the chair, and finds a large word in a dialogue balloon. He carefully spells the word, as he has heard his brother do.

"What does 'a-a-w-o-o-w-a-h!' mean?"

At my request James repeats the spelling. I figure it is the sound of a siren and tell him so, but he says it's not. He shows the picture to me. The word in question is the wailing of a Belgian Jew who knows he'll be killed in the morning. I tell James it means the mouse is sad. Eventually James concludes that the mice are going to jail for not wearing their hats.

At supper, Sam is still thinking about *Maus.* He is a serious boy, prone to prolonged pondering. He wants to be a scientist when he grows up.

"I'm glad there was a Hitler," he says.

"Why?" I say.

"Because if he hadn't lived, Grandma and Grandpa wouldn't go to New York and have Mommy. Then you wouldn't have met her. And there'd be no me. I have to be glad, see?"

I stare at him, awed by the practicality of his logic. He is an implacable child, a careful thinker. For me to present a counterargument is to attack his very being, deny his existence in the same way the Nazis tried to deny the Jews.

Hot Rod to Haldeman

Rita and I decided to picnic in my hometown of Haldeman with sandwiches and bottles of cold L-8, Kentucky's only native soft drink. Its official name is Ale-8-1, or "a late one," because it arrived on the market after Coca-Cola. L-8 is affectionately called swamp water or mule piss, and must be drunk cold from a long-neck bottle clamped between your thighs while driving.

I drove the Malibu with my left arm draped out the window in true country style. A large sign proclaimed the future site of a country club and an exclusive golf community. Trees were cut down and roads laid out. New houses clung to denuded slopes as if dropped from the sky. The entire enterprise reminded me of a trailer court for the affluent. "HickorY PointE," proclaimed a sign in large letters. If you squinted, they formed a new word—HYPE.

In Morehead I pointed out to Rita where I'd bought my first bike and shot my first game of pool. I know the eight miles between town and Haldeman better than I know the face of either of my sons. I know the shadows of the land, the stone outcroppings high on the hillside, the silhouette of the tree line at dusk. As we drove, I gave Rita a running commentary on the road—the two straight stretches where you could pass a slow car, the tobacco warehouse, the turn up Christy Creek where the old drive-in movie theater was built on a landfill. Now it's gone and a new grade school sits there. I stopped at Big Perry Road and told her about the school bus wreck. Farther on was Little Perry Road, a long dead-end hollow that followed a creek in classic Appalachian style.

The sky was so crisp and taut you expected it to snap in the wind. The leaves of a silver maple turned their bellies to the breeze and the tree looked covered with snow. We passed Gates, a community reduced to a railroad whistle post. At Hay's Branch I made the turn to Hay's Crossing, and showed Rita where a bunch of us boys once swam naked in a shallow muddy pool. One of us cut his foot on glass. A boy threw someone's shoes into the water. Somebody cried and somebody got mad. I couldn't remember which boy I had been.

It was not the land that Rita enjoyed, nor the stories of my past, but the Malibu. The throbbing engine thrilled her. She loved its speed and power. She sprawled luxuriously in the front seat, and said she'd lived in New York apartments that were smaller. The term *muscle car* came from the tremendous horsepower harnessed beneath the hood of cars in the late sixties and early seventies. Manufacturers in Detroit upped the ante until they were putting race cars on the street—Chevelle, GTO, Charger, Barracuda. Rowan County muscle cars were jacked up in the back with mag wheels. Large speakers sat in the rear seat wired to eight-track tape players bolted beneath the dash. A roach clip on a feather hung from the rearview mirror. Some drivers draped a flag in the back window—a Jolly Roger, the Stars and Bars, Kentucky's seal of the Commonwealth, a peace sign, or a giant marijuana leaf. People held drag races in Haldeman and across the county in the community of Farmers. Cars would burn rubber and fly low. Lucky boys drove them to high school, where everyone admired each other's ride in the parking lot. I rode the bus from farthest out in the county. I didn't own a car and the family rig was a yellow Volkswagen squareback that was severely embarrassing.

We sped past the ball diamond and voting house in the widest spot between the creek and the road. This was

Haldeman proper—the woods, two hollows, a creek, three hills, and dirt roads connected by animal paths. To reach a neighbor's house by car meant driving out your ridge and off your hill, following the creek to their hill, driving up it to their ridge. Walking through the woods was much quicker. Fifty years ago, the company store became the Haldeman post office, its flag fastened permanently to a pole that the postmaster, Avanelle Eldridge, carried outside every morning and belted to a fence post. At night she moved the flagpole inside. During winter, Avanelle heated the post office with a woodstove, until the government closed the facility.

At the top of the next hill was the county line, where the bootlegger sold beer, wine, and whiskey. His shack was abandoned. I bought my first whiskey there, saying it was for my father. I eased the big Malibu around the building, and made the turn toward Molten Hollow.

As a kid, I walked through the woods to Haldeman's only business, George's General Store. The air smelled of floor oil. You could sit in an old leather chair by the woodstove and drink pop forever. Three refrigerators stood against one wall, and everyone knew the contents—eggs and milk in one; bottles of pop in another; baloney, cheese, mustard, and mayonnaise in the last. Hand-hewn shelves held light bread, Vienna sausages, and dusty cans of soup.

To get there, you walked a dirt road along the ridge and descended a weedy path to the creek below. You followed another dirt road to the hardtop and crossed it to a creek. Searching its bank invariably produced enough pop bottles to trade for candy. I remembered Mom sending me for cigarettes but the store was closed. I crossed the swaybacked board that spanned the banks. George's wife answered the door and said they were eating supper. She handed me the store key in exchange for the money, saying she'd give me the change when I returned the key.

Nine years ago I saw George's cash register in the window of an antique store in town. I stared at it, remembering how the money drawer remained perpetually open. Now it is shut forever. When I think of George's, I'm not recalling the actual event, but the last time I remembered it. In this fashion memory reclaims itself like land after a fire.

I showed Rita my grade school, built of enormous chunks of stone. So few children complete high school that the grade school offered an elaborate graduation ceremony with cap and gown, pomp and circumstance. My proudest day was being selected as valedictorian of my eighth-grade class. Past the school we followed Bearskin Creek up Bearskin Hollow along Bearskin Road, which crisscrossed the creek according to terrain. I took Rita to the top of the ridge near New Sill Graveyard where I first smoked a cigarette. I tried to explain my desire to visit a dead town, surrounded by evidence of its former glory. Haldeman flourished during the 1920s—boasting a train station, high school, saloon, barbershop, public gardens, tennis court, even plumbing and a baseball team. Beneath the humped hills were thick veins of unique clay that made hard bricks. Their ability to withstand enormous heat made them ideal for building kilns in the factories up north. The Haldeman Brickyard was the biggest employer in the region. Then Mr. Haldeman sold the town and moved away.

When I grew up, the town consisted of two hundred unemployed people. My grade school held a huge trophy case won by the high school that had been shut down sixty years before. Old railroad tracks traversed the land. Yellow bricks emblazoned with the name "Haldeman" reminded every child that our hometown had once mattered. Now it was like the bricks—broke and crumbling, embedded in the past.

Rita and I drove up my home hill. I stopped at a slight plateau, where the old path cut through the woods, now grown over with weeds, indecipherable from the brush and saplings. I continued past the Gob Dump, a gray substance on which nothing grew, evidence of a long empty mine. I played kickball at the hilltop, using a low clay-dirt hill for first base, the tip of a buried rock for second, a locust branch as third. Home plate was a vague area of shade. One ridge road held the house I grew up in, where my parents still lived. Other roads held the Henderson homeplace, Randy's trailer and woodshop, Faron's old trailer, the Sam Bowen house now empty and in disrepair, Dixie Blizzard's old place presently occupied by people from off, the Fraley man who moved here from Carter County thirty years ago and was still regarded as a stranger although his sons were Haldeman boys, and the Hortons' old place now occupied by one of the Messer boys, whose family had lived on the hill longer than anyone. I was home. The roads were paved and the children gone.

I drove sedately down the hill to Buffalo Hollow. The road tightened and turned to gravel, then dirt, and finally became twin ruts with grass between. I parked the Malibu in a wide spot and cut the engine. Rita scooted close to me. I explained the history of Buffalo Hollow as a site for romance. She told me she was glad I'd brought her here.

On the way home we played Lynyrd Skynyrd on the car stereo. Rita sat beside me on the bench seat, exactly as I'd hoped a girl would sit twenty years ago. I kissed her at a traffic light. When the color turned green, I chirped a black mark on Main Street. Rita laughed and put her feet on the dashboard. We drove through town in five minutes. We stopped by the grade school and picked up our kids and took them to the Dairy Queen for dilly bars.

Arthur Becomes a Handyman

The boss wants to paint his room. I think maybe I get a piece of grub out of this and I said, yeah, I can paint. He had something that looked like a brush. I wasn't sure what it was, a brush or a broom, but you could see through it. He had old paint. I started to mix them but the paint would separate. I had some violet in there, some red, some yellow and it became streaky. I was able to finish that room in two days. He came in and I said, waugh, there's not enough paint, so I modernized it a little.

He was very impressed. It looked like marble when it dried out. He said, what else can you do? I said, I do carpentry. So I made a desk for him. I put some legs on a bureau top and I polished it nicely. He came into the machine shop and he never saw a more beautiful piece of furniture than that. He said, you do very well. From a man like this, it was like getting a million dollars. He was shooting people for much less.

Now came my biggest prize. I said, if you give me the equipment, I can put light in the main warehouse. We go with wire from one side of the camp to the other side and we got light. He was happy. I was his personal handyman after that.

He had a favorite man in the Jewish Police. I called him sergeant. He had a white shirt, whiter than white, and he was the object of envy. Nice uniform, clean hands, smelled like a rose. The sergeant had a beautiful head of hair. The prisoners were unshaven at this particular point. Their hair was long and they looked like slobs. So the boss said, get those prisoners cleaned up. I want everybody to shave their hair, shave completely. Everybody, you included, he tells his friend the sergeant in front of us.

The sergeant is asking for permission to leave his hair on. The boss said, oh sure. You have a beautiful head of hair. I would never dream to deprive you of this beautiful head of hair. And he turns around, and shoots the sergeant in the back of the head.

He tells everybody to take the body and bring him over there. And he led the whole procession to the dump where we have our garbage. He says, now we gonna bury this beautiful Jew. We threw him in the garbage and there was rotting potatoes and all kind of shit. He says, everybody kneel and say a prayer for this beautiful man. Everybody kneels at the dump. He goes from one guy to another guy and says, are you praying? Are you praying? Do you pray? Now bury the sonofabitch.

That was my boss.

Irene Sees Beno

They took Arthur to one camp and Beno and me to the different camp. There were big cars for the transport of animals. Beno and me wind up in Plaszow. Arthur had a better camp.

I saw Beno. He was fourteen. He grew so much, I could not believe it. Beno was a short little guy, he grew to six feet. They took him from Plaszow after a year. He was sixteen. I don't know where Beno went and I never heard from him and Arthur he feels guilty. It's his nature that he blames himself. We don't know where he was and where he died.

Losing Beno was worse for Arthur than his father and mother. That he was not taking care of his little brother. Like Sam would feel guilty that he didn't take care of James. It's a terrible feeling. I was lucky enough that I didn't really have guilt. My mother, I saved her for three months. I could not do more than I did.

Soup Beans and Corn Bread

I had lunch with my mother at the Dixie Grill. It was unusual for us to have a private meal, one of the rare times when I saw her actually eat. My mother attended MSU for two decades, and now worked for a nonlitigating lawyer, an old family friend. Her job included greeting people as they entered his office. She had never held a job when I lived here, and it pleased me to take my mother out during her lunch break.

The Dixie Grill is a small room filled with tables and chairs—no booths. When my mother and I entered, everyone looked to see who we were. We followed etiquette by sweeping the area with our vision and settling on someone to smile at. People never feel hurt if you don't wave to them personally. They understand that you are merely obeying custom by showing the crowd that you're not a snob. All of this is surreptitious of course, with no sense of choreography or awareness. It's simple convention. Staring is not considered rude here. In fact, the opposite is true—failing to acknowledge someone is a much worse social gaffe. Staring at strangers is common because you must try to figure out who the person is related to, if you know the family, and if you are perhaps distant kin. One of these scenarios holds true, because there are no strangers in the hills. People don't come here unless they are visiting relatives.

The Dixie Grill's menu is traditional mountain fare—fried, fatty, starchy, and sweet. There is no designated smoking section, which is to say the entire restaurant is a smoking section. My mother and I ordered the daily special of soup beans, mixed greens, and corn bread. To eat properly, you douse the damp clump of greens with vinegar, and crumble your corn bread into your soup beans. We looked at each other across the table. My mother seemed to enjoy the idea of eating lunch with me more than the actual experience.

"How are the boys?" she said.

"Pretty good. Sam's not too happy with school."

"You always liked school."

I ate a bite of soggy corn bread.

"Are things all right with you," I said.

"Great."

"And Dad?"

"Great."

"How about the house?" I said. "The new roof?"

"Great. I'm so glad you're here. This is the busiest time of the busiest restaurant in Morehead."

"Great," I said.

There were perhaps twenty tables in the room, four of which were empty. My mother kept glancing around to see who saw us together. Other people were likewise engaged, which slowed the pace of eating. Many people were there merely to be seen—businesspeople communicating liaisons to the world, couples showing everyone that their marital problems were repaired, bosses eating with employees to display good relations. No one lunched alone at the Dixie Grill.

A boy I'd grown up with came by the table to say hello. He was balding now and I remembered when a VISTA worker took him to a dentist. The next day he brought a toothbrush to school. Since he'd never seen one, he figured none of us had either. I inquired about his six brothers and four sisters. He worked at Guardian, the only industry around, a manufacturer of ball bearings. They tried to unionize but failed. He still lived in Haldeman, but was thinking of moving.

"They built that new school," he said, "but it ain't the

same," he said. "They combined Haldeman and Elliotville, and make those babies ride a bus twelve miles. Parents don't go to PTA meetings because it's too far away."

"Don't they use the school for anything?"

"To vote in. They closed the voting house. But they're going to open it again because so many people quit voting when they changed it."

"Why'd they close the voting house?"

"No bathroom," he said. "The state says you got to have a bathroom. Shoot, there's some folks would vote just to use the bathroom."

I laughed and he returned to his table. My mother smiled brightly to a person across the room.

"You know, Chris," my mother said. "I liked it better when you lived in Albuquerque."

"What?"

"I could visit."

I continued to nod, my head slowly moving like a marionette in the wind. To reach the rest room I had to step into a narrow hall at the rear of the restaurant. The men's room was occupied. I glanced around and quickly went into the women's room, where I splashed cold water on my face and wrists. As I emerged, an older woman was slowly coming through the door. She stared at me, utterly aghast to find a man in the ladies' room. She was a retired high school teacher and she withered me with a look, shaking her head as if to say, "Christopher, you may have gone off and come back, but you have not grown up one bit."

I paid the bill and said hello to my freshman composition teacher from college. I nodded to a man I'd once bought marijuana from. I opened the door for my high school typing teacher, a woman I held in high esteem.

I walked my mother back to her job at a new building that had formerly housed a Laundromat. She smiled at the door, resuming her role as a sixty-five-year-old employee in an olive skirt, the ubiquitous green of a redhead. Her hair was a different color now, but her taste in clothes was the same. She thanked me for lunch, straightened her skirt, lifted her chin, and gave me the smile of a receptionist seeing a person out. She nodded once and turned away. I watched the door close after her.

I realized that I knew very little about my mother's life, and that lunch had offered no insight. I didn't even know if she was happy. I hoped that my coming home would allow her to open herself to me. She never talked of her childhood and had told me nothing of her mother. I don't even know my grandmother's name. She died young.

When I was a child, some wild boys drove a hot rod along the dirt road on our hill. It was jacked-up in the back with short pipes that produced a rhythmic roar. A large black swastika was painted on each door. I had never seen that symbol before. I thought the car was cool, the driver was cool, the loud music roaring was cool. I especially thought the swastika was cool. For some reason I decided to carve it into the lid of a wooden box on my mother's dresser. I was about ten years old. I used the sharp end of a diaper pen. When my father asked if I had done it, I said yes and told him about the car. He said the box had belonged to my grandmother. It was the only item my mother had from her. I never saw the box again.

Arthur Finds a Friend

There were women working in camp also that came from the outside. I met this woman and she told me she worked in a restaurant. She was from the same city as I was. She was a pretty girl. Simple but crazy. She said to me, why don't you say to your boss over there I am a good cook.

So I said to my boss, maybe you want a good cook here. Maybe somebody want to cook a good meal for you.

He said, do you know her?

I said, ya, ya, she's a good cook.

So she cooked him a meal. It was good and he hired her as an official cook for him. She came every day and the next thing I know, she sleeps with him. She wants to stay in the camp and there's a house adjacent. Nobody lives there. We used it mostly for storage. I tell the boss, why don't we fix the house up, you could have a nice house there. So he gave me a couple of men. I paint and fix and put electric wiring in. A bathroom I make.

She moved in with him. He made her chief of providing all the supplies from there to us. The woman, she's not a friend of mine anymore. She orders me around like a big shot. She is the lady with her slave. She goes sometimes to the other camp where my wife is. I said to her, do me a favor and give my wife my bread. She tells me, ya, I leave it. I said, how's my wife? She said, fine. I found out after the war she's playing games with me, she doesn't do this. I thought that my wife got the food. She didn't. My wife never got anything. It was the only time I was happy, and it was not real.

My friend the woman, she orders me around all over the place. She's in the bathtub. She orders me, wash my back. Wash my feet. I prepare coffee for her in the morning. I did everything for her. She constantly tells me to come in the morning, and if I don't come in the morning, I'll be a dead Jew in the afternoon.

I don't want to make her angry because she gets drunk and is totally irresponsible. I tried to appease her. I've never been as nice to anybody as I was to that girl. My boss knows that I go there. I have a feeling that he knows something is all wrong, because every time she calls the office, he calls me on a loudspeaker. Go up to my house and fix something. I think one day he gonna come in. Because if she tells me to wash her back, I'm gonna wash her back and he gonna come in and shoot me right there.

He abused her a lot. He used to get drunk and beat her up. She had cigarette burns on her body. I would find her in bad condition, bloody and semi-conscious. I put her in the bathtub, put some warm water in it, and she just sat there crying a lot. She would get herself together again and do what he told her to do.

I felt very bad because I blamed myself that she wound up in this position. She wasn't too old, maybe a couple years older than me. And she always said that she was gonna kill him. She said before the war is ended and her parents gonna find out about her living with the German, she gonna burn that place down. After the war, I met a friend of mine and he said this place was burned down.

She suffered a lot and I have a bad feeling that if I would be dead, maybe she would not wind up like that.

Poetry Saves Irene

We had a poetry group behind the latrine. We got together from the same barracks with Elona Carmel. She started the whole group. I don't know her married name. We gathered together behind the toilets, where we were safe. Each one prepared something. We had pieces of paper from me because I worked in the paper factory. Elona wrote a poem and we listened, and then each one, whatever they could deliver, a poem, some thoughts, some hopes, some descriptions. When I think back, this is like a little sunshine opening.

It was not allowed to do that. That was taking a chance, but we did. These little gatherings made a big difference and I was not taken. I was not destroyed. Maybe outside, but not mentally. Poetry saved me.

Harley in a Car

Appalachia suffers from "brain-drain," in which the bright and ambitious people depart and seldom return. Those left behind tend to perpetuate the social problems that forced folks out in the first place. People who leave crave the opportunity to assimilate by erasing their accent, speaking vaguely about hometowns, and embrace the trappings of a new life. Many tend to hide who they are and where they are from. I had been through this myself.

For the first time in two decades, I could stand in a room full of people as a member of the majority. My favorite class was Intro to Creative Writing because of the sense of freedom young people brought to their work. The top two students, Eugene and Sandra, were in the class. Eugene arrived early to return the books I'd lent him—Flannery O'Connor and Breece D'J Pancake—writers from rural worlds.

"I never read nothing like those," Eugene said. "In high school, we read *Romeo and Juliet,* the biggest bunch of bullshit you ever did see."

"I know what you mean," I said. "Two teenagers in love and their folks mad at them. Families feuding with each other. People saying one thing and meaning another. Getting killed for no reason. Nothing like where I grew up. What about you?"

"Well," he said as a grin slid along his smooth jaw. "I know what you're doing. But we never had swordfights up my hollow. And we don't talk funny, either."

"Let me tell you something, Eugene. You might not think you talk funny, but the minute you step foot out of these hills, everyone else will think so. Next time you read Shakespeare, just substitute guns for swords. The best thing, though, is to read what you want to."

"Got one for me?"

"Still want short stories?"

"Yup."

I gave him books by Mary Hood and Larry Brown.

"Georgia and Mississippi," I said. "Talk about talking funny."

He slipped the books in his bag. Students flowed around me, the twang of their accent bouncing off the concrete walls. The day's assignment involved reading a poem that used the word *waning.* Sandra said she didn't know the word.

"You're an English major," I said. "This is a writing class. When you don't know a word, you should look it up."

"I can't look up every word I don't know," she said.

"Sure you can, Sandra. In fact, you're supposed to. That's how you learn new words. I know one guy who makes a mark by a word he looks up so he can know if he's searched for it before."

"Well, I went to school in the hills," she said. "There's a lot of words I don't know."

"I understand."

"Since you're from the hills, you should give me a break."

"No way," I said. "That's even more reason not to give you or anyone else a break. You can't think that way. That's buying into the whole victim status we've been given. The federal government thinks that way and they throw money at the problem. This college tells new faculty that the students are a 'special population.' Do you know what that means? It means they don't expect anything from you. Once you think you deserve special treatment simply because of who you are, you're in a lot of trouble. You are then participating in your own subjugation. As long as we act like dumb hillbillies, people will always see us that way.

The stereotype comes from within the culture, not from outside! We must defy the expectations, not feed them! We cannot voluntarily participate in our own social oppression!"

Out of breath, I stopped and looked at the faces of the students. Some were visibly upset. Others showed the familiar glazed expression of having turned inward for protection. I realized that my yelling was in itself a form of oppression.

"Class dismissed," I said. "Go look up the word *subjugation.* I'm sorry I yelled."

The class left silently, no one remaining behind. I walked out of the building, thinking that I was the same as a father being cruel to show cruelty was wrong, or a boss belittling workers to increase morale, or a preacher judging his flock. I had just behaved in a way that I had always despised.

Sandra was waiting on the sidewalk outside the English building, an expression on her face of shame and dismay. She wanted to talk in private and we walked half a block to my office.

"I lied," she said.

"What do you mean?"

"About why I didn't look up that word. I don't have a dictionary, Chris. I'm sorry, but I don't have one. I never saw one except in school. I don't even know where to get one."

"You can get one in a bookstore."

"I've never even been in a bookstore, Chris, not a real one. They don't have one where I'm from. The college bookstore is just textbooks and T-shirts. I'm sorry, but it's true."

"How old are you?"

"Going on twenty."

"Well, you're on the same track as me, Sandra. I went to my first bookstore when I was nineteen. I had to leave to find one, too."

"Morehead's where I left for."

"It was the first step for me. Maybe you can go a little farther."

"I've thought about it," she said, "but I don't have any idea where."

She stood to leave. I grabbed the dictionary from my desk, a hardback College Edition, and offered it to her.

"Please," I said. "I want you to have it."

She took the heavy book. Her lips pressed together and her eyes got wet.

"Thank you," she said. "No one ever did anything like this for me."

"You deserve it, Sandra."

She nodded and turned away, then spun back and gave me a quick hug, the dictionary between our bodies. She hurried from the office. I sat for a long time, realizing how ignorant I was of my students' needs. The first lesson was mine, not theirs.

I gathered my classwork in a daze, and headed for the old Malibu at Mrs. Jayne's house.

A car stopped in the street beside me. People here don't use their horns, and think nothing of halting traffic to talk with someone. Harley grinned at me, his scarred face missing a few teeth, his hair already gray as an old fence post. I hadn't seen him since the first day of school, when he invited me to get high with him in the woods.

Harley sat behind the wheel of a rusty car. He appeared happy and proud, and I opened the door and got in. I couldn't recall ever seeing Harley in the driver's seat. It was utterly incongruous, like finding a chain saw in an Easter basket. The car ashtray overflowed with cigarette butts. On the transmission hump was a large table ashtray, also full to overflowing.

"Want a cigarette?" he said.

I told him I quit and asked about the car. He explained that he gave up drinking after twenty years, and the car belonged to his girlfriend. She's the first girlfriend he's ever had, a Caudill. This last name was as common in the hills as tree leaves, and Harley took pains to identify her. Such distinctions are crucial in Rowan County, where people will judge you forever by who you dated ten years back. They shoot friends and neighbors over these issues.

"She ain't one of them hollow Caudills from up sixty," he said. "And she ain't out of that black-headed bunch on the creek. She might be kin to that uppity bunch, you know the ones, but she don't claim it."

Harley told me her mother's last name, which I vaguely recognized. Essentially, he was letting me know that his girlfriend was a solid middle-of-the-road Caudill, neither inbred nor rich, either of which is highly suspect. Her only indiscretion was having married a man from Martin County who left her after she bore his triplets, one of whom died shortly after birth. People used her as an example of the sort of cosmic penalty that is inflicted for marrying out of the county. There are no coincidences here. Everything is governed by cause and effect.

Harley was still talking. His girlfriend did everything for him.

"I don't even have to light a cigarette, Chris. She lights it and puts it in my mouth for me. She's got something to eat any time of the day or night. She won't let me take a bath. She just warshes me off cleaner than I've ever been. Dries me, too."

"You look clean," I said.

"Son, when we're out she don't look at nobody else. She clings to me like a monkey. She's fat and ugly but I don't care."

Harley had recently moved ten miles away from Haldeman across the county line. It was foreign territory to him, like Montana or New York for me. He felt the same as I did about the changes in the county. Our hometown was nothing but dirt and houses.

"Ain't it awful how they done Morehead," he said. "I'd not live here for ten dollars a day. They've got Main Street bent like a bobby pin. And son, Haldeman's gone, just gone. It's like our backyard got took away."

Our agreement on loss made perfect sense to Harley. It meant nothing that I had traveled half a million miles to his ten, that we both quit drinking, that we hadn't seen each other in many years. All that mattered was having grown up together. No one can ever know a Haldeman boy like another Haldeman boy. I admired his car for a while.

"Shoot," he said, "I just got my license two months ago. Had to borrow a car to take it in, and got it on my first try. First try, son! You got anywhere you need to go? I'll drive you wherever. It don't matter how far or how long it takes. I got gas and everything. You just tell me where to point this rig. I'll take care of the rest."

I realized that Harley wanted to return years of favors to people who drove him around the county. His glee was palpable. The old Pinto looked like it would barely get out of a driveway, but in eastern Kentucky, a car's appearance could be extremely deceiving, evidenced by my Malibu. I didn't have the heart to show my car to him. It would feel too much like bragging, and I wanted Harley to enjoy his own satisfaction.

I declined his offer to go somewhere.

"That's all right," Harley said. "We'll set and smoke. Only I forgot you quit. Well, I'll smoke double then."

He lit two cigarettes and smoked them simultaneously while recalling various car wrecks, two of which I was in as a teenager. There was a time when several of us boys got drunk and deliberately wrecked cars for the fun of it. I remembered getting stoned on pot with him shortly before I left Kentucky the first time. Harley was astonished at my decision, and said, "There's nowhere in the world I'd rather live than Haldeman."

He told me of driving to visit his brother in Huntington, West Virginia, three hours away. Everyone warned him against such an undertaking—his family, his friends, the various counselors who'd attempted to look after him, even the police. No one believed in Harley. I realized that Sandra had lied in class because no one had taught her to believe in herself. I thought of Eugene's periodic despair over deserting his county for college. My own efforts at self-belief wavered constantly.

I asked Harley if he'd been scared of the trip to Huntington.

"Shit fire and save matches," he said. "I've got a car and a map and a set of eyeballs. Drove right there. Stopped once for gas. Never made a wrong turn but the one time and I was right by my brother's house when I done it."

He finished a cigarette, and contemplated the second one still burning in his other hand.

"You seem like you're doing good," I said.

"I'm happy as a whore in a pecker patch."

He hit me in the arm and laughed. Abruptly he looked down, as if talking to his lap.

"Son, I had no idea what a man could do if he wasn't in the habit of drinking."

"What made you quit?" I said.

"Thought I was going to die of it. What happened was I had me a hangover that went for a week. Never got no better. I couldn't eat or sleep. Every water I took came right back. They was puke bags laying thick around my bed. So I just decided I was done with it. I didn't want to die. Not before I got my license, anyhow. You sure you don't want me to drive you somewhere."

"Okay," I said, "drive me around the block."

He very carefully put his foot on the brake, turned the key, and slid the automatic shifter to reverse. He looked both ways twice. He checked his mirrors, placed his right arm on the back of my seat, peered over his shoulder, and eased into the street. A cop drove by, one of the few in town, and Harley waved.

"He don't know what to think," Harley said. "I've knowed him a long time."

He executed a perfect reverse turn, shifted gears, and

began moving forward at five miles per hour. I was reminded of teaching Rita to drive on these very roads a decade back. She still drove like Harley did now—shoulders high, neck pronged forward, hands tense on the wheel, staring straight ahead. My sons told me that on long trips, they remind her to breathe. I understood why Harley's girlfriend lit cigarettes for him in the car.

We circled the block at a funereal pace. Harley held the wheel with his hands clenched tight. We saw one car the entire drive and Harley became extremely tense, veins rising like cords on his forearms. He didn't relax until the car went by in the opposite direction. He triple-checked the mirror to guarantee clearance.

He parked and I reminded myself to breathe. Harley was grinning in a new way that was also an old way, draining years from his face, erasing the marks of alcohol, cigarettes, bad food, incarceration. He was not a forty-five-year-old alcoholic on the mend, and I wasn't his neighbor who left for work and came back home. We were two Haldeman boys on the loose. Anything might happen. If we spent the night in the pokey, we'd laugh in the morning. If we wrecked the car, we'd cover it up with bushes and walk home through the woods. I was proud of Harley, and happy for him, but if you're a man in eastern Kentucky, you can't go around saying you love other men. We communicated through our cars, our fists, and the ancient go-between of women.

I hit him in the shoulder.

"You're a good driver," I said. "I bet you could go anywhere you wanted to. Farther than West Virginia even."

"You reckon?"

"I know it."

I opened the door and placed a boot on the cement.

"Chris," he said.

I turned my head three-quarters. His grin had faded and the years returned, but he was still Harley. He looked hard at me. I didn't know what was coming. It might be anything—an offer to smoke a joint or drink some whiskey, a request for a loan, a punch in the face.

"Haldeman was nice, wasn't it," he said.

"Yes," I said.

"I got to where I had to leave there."

"I know, Harley. Me, too."

"Sometimes I miss it."

I left the car and hurried away and hid behind a tree. I leaned around it like I had a hundred times with Harley as a boy in the woods. He lifted his chin in a wave. His hands were on the wheel, a cigarette in his mouth. He shifted the car into gear. He slowly backed the car into the street, stopping every five feet to check both ways.

I understood why people were afraid of him heading to Huntington on his own. I also understood how the liberty of departure gave him confidence. In Morehead, Harley drove the way everyone expected him to drive, but I suspected he had driven differently on his way to West Virginia. Like me, he had to leave to defy expectations. If Sandra left the hills, I felt sure she'd look up words she didn't know.

Arthur Volunteers for a Concentration Camp

I have a chance to go to the camp where my wife is. I volunteer to go but the day before I arrive, they evacuated my wife. I am the only person in the war who volunteered for concentration camp.

Plaszow is where my worst is. Whatever bad happened to me physically happened there. And it was bad for many reasons. It was the same city I was born in. People who used to be my friends treat me not so good. There was a gallows, a whipping place, and a shooting place. Each a different type of punishment. I didn't know for what you got beaten, for what you got hung, for what you got shot. I wasn't interested. They shaved us. A very short crew cut. But to give us a little oomph, they shaved a stripe down the middle of the crew cut. You could recognize a prisoner right away.

Shooting people was a daily occurrence. I was working on an electric pole one day and it was a desolated part of the camp, on the outskirts. A beautiful day. The countryside is lush. I was working and I saw this car, a Mercedes, stop and a very elegant lady came out of it with a German officer. They walked with a little girl. It was often the case, some of the very pretty women, Jewish women, wound up with the German officers. She had a nice fur coat. I didn't see her face. She took a walk with him and he shot the girl and then he shot her. He drove the car away. I continue working on the electric pole.

They put me in with a group of electricians from Kraków and they don't like me. They sent me into the worst places, for instance, to fix things for the commander of the camp. He is Goeth, a complete lunatic. He rides a white horse with his lover to the camp at sunrise. A beautiful woman with long hair. He had these stallions, riding around the camp. He is from Vienna. Very tall, a beautiful man. Looks like something out of an Aryan opera. Something not quite earthly. He has two dogs running with him all the time, killers these dogs.

Goeth loved to shoot people for any kind of reason. He would go to the women's camp where they peeled potatoes and he would say, ladies, please do your work, and he'd go around this mound of potatoes, and say, this is a beautiful child, this is a beautiful child. She doesn't deserve this. She deserves better. So he shot her. After the war, Goeth's defense is he had to be cruel to stay in command because if Berlin knew he was soft on the Jews, they would replace him. To save Jews, he had to be harsh.

He has a magnificent little villa on top of the camp, and a lot of Hungarian girls working for him. There's a whole operation going on. He has a beautiful garden with elegant lights and a piano. Best wines, best liquor, classical music all the time. I love it when the electricians send me to the villa because the girls give me food. The electricians are sending me there because Goeth is crazy and might shoot me, but I'm getting food. I want to go there. They think I'm the crazy one, not Goeth!

The electric iron doesn't work and I can't fix it. Time is done with it. The light is coming from the ceiling and a shadow is in my eyes. I turn around, and Goeth was standing over me. He said, does it work?

The only thing I can do is make believe. I push this wire in, put the screws in the thing. Nothing explodes. Suddenly it works for a minute. I am saved.

I had the pleasure to look into his eyes and if I ever saw the Devil looking at me, it was him because his eyes were as cold as steel. I had this heavy iron. I could have certainly hurt him badly. I could have hit him at least twice. He was hanged after the war, but I could have killed him. Death was liberating for him. You cannot hurt or demean somebody who's dead. Him and Hitler should have been sentenced to life in prison under the same conditions as me.

Irene Stays Healthy

It was terrible, because you never knew from day to day what was the next for us. Everybody was for themselves. I got used to it, everybody gets used to it when you have to. It was not so terrible anymore. The food was not so bad but a lot of people froze to death.

I didn't let myself go like some people. They got overridden by lice and by pimples. They didn't look like humans. I exchanged one week of bread for a little comb and a mirror. That was my black market. I had it all the time. Nobody else used it. The lice was very bad but I didn't have lice. I cut my hair myself for style a little. And my uniform I make nicer. Always I try to look a little good. I am still very vain.

I tried to help people in little ways. I made dresses from burlap sacks so they look healthy. It was important to look healthy. If not, to the clinic and you die. In camp you want them to think you are healthy. I exchange my potatoes for beets, and I use the beets to rub on my face for color. I look a little better. This I do for the others who aren't so good. Who are maybe a little sick. Beets. It makes good color of the cheek.

After the war I met a woman on the Pitkin Avenue in Brooklyn. She is hugging and crying and saying I am an angel. She tells this to Rita. I am not an angel. I did terrible things. I was lucky.

Dirty Money

Sometimes I worry if I can pull this off. I leave my writing desk in tears. Will people care that a gentile is writing about the Holocaust? Am I appropriating Jewish material? Am I respectful enough? Why am I doing it in the first place? The questions continue endlessly, the writer's self-torture at three A.M. There were no Jews where I grew up. As a kid I thought they were the same as Christians only they went to church on Saturday. I married the first Jew I met.

I remember a local woman whose husband beat her repeatedly for twenty years. He once shot her brother for trying to protect her. After that no one bothered the couple again. He eventually beat her so badly that she was hospitalized for several weeks and he went to prison. The husband was released a broken man, having aged hard in every way. His wife suffered brain damage from his last beating and required significant care. Because neither of them could work, the state sent them a monthly check, a form of welfare that reminded me of war reparations.

I call Arthur and ask if he has looked into compensation. The subject pisses him off mightily.

"No," he says. "I have no interest in money from the Germans or the Poles. My wife says take the money and give it to the kids. Let the grandchildren go to college. On what, I ask you? On the lives of their great-grandparents? If a murderer pays me money for killing my brother, it makes me dirty. You pay twenty-five dollars, twenty-five thousand dollars, two hundred fifty thousand dollars—then you're okay. You've paid off your debt. And what after they pay me off? What do I tell my mother and father if I should see them in Heaven? Hi mother, they paid me off. They paid me off! That money is dirty. That money is fricking dirty.

"And Sonny, I know them. They are cheapskates. If they pay me back wages for slave labor, they will charge me room and board for concentration camp."

Jimmy Joe at the Video

The other day a man in the video store reminded me that we knew each other thirty years ago. His name was engraved on a small oval of polished brass attached to his belt near the buckle. The last time I saw Jimmy Joe his hair hung past his shoulders. He played guitar in the county's only rock band, drove a red GTO, and had girlfriends galore.

"Since you left," Jimmy Joe said, "I got married and divorced three times. Right now I want a wife that runs around on me. That way she ain't bothering me at home."

"My wife don't bother me much."

"See there, probably is running around."

"Think I should ask her?" I said.

"You really want to know if she is?"

"Don't reckon," I said. "Long as she comes home, it's her life, ain't it."

"Son, you always was smart." Jimmy Joe lowered his voice, and glanced rapidly around to ensure privacy. "You want to burn one out back?"

"No," I said. "Pot doesn't do for me what I want done anymore."

"That's downheartening," he said. "What is it you want done, Chris?"

"I don't know. I tried everything and nothing did a good enough job. I quit all of it."

"Maybe it's you."

"You're pretty smart, too, Jimmy Joe. What are you up to these days? Still playing guitar? You were the best around."

"Had to put it down, son. Just gave up on it. Went to barber school and moved to Lexington, but came back home."

"How come?" I said.

"Too many heads to cut."

"Too many?"

"Yes, it's a big town and I like to do the same thing over and over. Same job, same heads, same food. Shoot, I'm here renting the same movie for the hundredth time. I'd save money buying it off of them."

"What movie?"

"*Taxi Driver.* Ever seen it?"

"It's a good one," I said. "You should get *Mean Streets.* Same guy made it. Same actor, too."

"No, got to rent this one. I love that Bickle, T. That's

what it says on the back of his jacket you know—Bickle, T. I got it stenciled on one of mine. I tried to get people to start calling me that, but it didn't work. You can't pick your own nickname. That's one of the rules. You ain't got a cigarette do you?"

"No, I quit."

"Me, too," he said. "But I ran out of nerve pills and figured I might as well smoke."

"You get nervous, Jimmy Joe?"

"As a cliff rat, son. As a cliff rat."

"I never heard of that kind."

"Me neither. But any rat that lives on a cliff would be nervous. See how my skin is kindly orange-colored?"

He pulled back his sleeve to show his arm, surprising me with its distinct orange hue. He turned his hands over.

"Palms, too," he said. "That's what normal skin is supposed to look like, son. It's from taking a lot of carotene. That's why they call carrots carrots, on account of the color. It's supposed to calm you down."

"I didn't know that."

"People are starting to get knowledged about it. You know, the Internet and whatnot."

"You're on the Internet?"

"Why, sure. Best thing that's come in here since town water. That e-mail cooks with gas, don't it."

"It's all right."

"All right? I figured you'd be all over that."

"Well," I said. "It bugs me sometimes. It's permanent as a letter, but spontaneous as a phone call. It's good to exchange information, but not communication."

"Son, you ain't changed a bit."

"Hey," I said. "You seen Harley around?"

"That's one old boy could use some carotene. I pity the world if Harley gets saved. He'll dry a river out and wear the preacher down. I got to go, son, I can't be dark getting home. Makes me nervous to drive at night."

"All right," I said. "See ya."

He strode away clutching the video. I envied Jimmy Joe for knowing exactly what he wanted—the comfort of familiarity. You can drive five hundred miles in any direction and eat the same food, put the same gas in your car, sleep at the same hotel, watch the same TV show, and admire the same bland print screwed to the wall. Freedom is terrifying. *Taxi Driver* is soothing.

Arthur Loses an Eye

The food dispersed to the prisoners was lousy. Sometimes the soup we got was decent. In the evening you could stand and get coffee. It wasn't really coffee, just black water, but it was hot. They take some corn, roast it, then brew it, and make coffee out of it. You could drink it. It tasted bitter, but it had some nutrients in it.

I am waiting to get coffee in a long line of prisoners standing in front of the kitchen. Naturally the Jewish Police were keeping order, so a guy wouldn't go twice for food. They're walking back and forth with whips, about six feet long, like for animals. Every so often the whip goes over the prisoner's head. Everybody knows that. We are standing and—pow—the end of the whip takes my eye. It came over the back of the head. The tip hit my eye. That's it. I was blind from then on.

The Worst Thing for Irene

The worst thing was being alone.

I was lucky. I was never beaten up. My finger was hit once with a hammer. Just for fun. I was working on something in the paper factory and I put my finger there, and he came and hit me. It broke the finger. It was not that I was punished. He was just playing. The hammer was laying there next to me so he picked it up and hit. I was not physically abused. But I saw killing, a lot of killing.

That was the worst thing.

College Students Now and Then

Two activities that give me genuine happiness are writing alone in a room and walking alone in the woods. In Kentucky I combined them by hiding a series of collapsible camp chairs among the trees. Each morning I walked a different route, moving from one chair to another. I also began writing longhand in small notebooks, exactly as I'd written many years before, recording prolonged journal entries about daily events. I had no plan, no hope, no motive to my writing. It was merely a habit that evolved into a discipline. I tried to write what came to mind. Sometimes I sat for hours without writing a single word.

The joy of nature is its constant reminder of how humans no longer belong. We can do nothing as perfect as a bird flying through the precise center of a small space between branches. Alone among the trees, I desire nothing. I try not to seek, which frees me to see what is revealed. Each day I empty the cistern of my mind and let the woods refill me. I want what is here to become who I am. I want to carry the secrets of the trees.

On the mornings I wrote in the woods, I entered the classroom wearing muddy boots and a plaid coat matted with burrs. Kentuckians were accustomed to the idea of walking in the woods as a necessary part of life. A few students told me they had followed my example and begun writing in the woods. One of these was Eugene, who often lingered after class.

"How you doing in your other classes," I said.

"All right, I reckon. Sometimes I don't think I'm cut out for school."

"I know the feeling. What are you cut out for?"

"Well, that's just it. I don't rightly know. Sometimes I can't stand to be at home, but I don't know where else to go. That's why I'm in school."

"There's the army and the Peace Corps. But the army makes you take orders and the Peace Corps wants a college degree."

"Sometimes I think about going to Ohio."

"You got people there?"

"Yeah, my mom's cousins are laying thick. They can get me on at them factories."

"Is that what you want?" I said.

"I don't know."

"A lot of people just want to stay right in these old hills and do what their daddy and their papaw did. Nothing wrong with that, either. I envy them. But you're not that way, Eugene. You want more. Me, too. The first thing is to find out what you don't want."

"Sometimes I don't want to think."

"That's a good way to get bad habits. What I do is write in my journal the things I don't want to think, and that way they're out of my head."

"I thought diaries were for girls." he said.

"Didn't you ever watch *Star Trek?* Remember how Captain Kirk has that star log? Well, he ain't a girl and neither am I."

"Well, you'd damn sure make an ugly one. Why don't you come home with me this weekend. See how we party up in Martin County."

"I don't know about that."

"I read your books so I know you ain't against getting a little wild. You didn't get saved here lately, did you?"

"Not hardly. I just ain't going to Martin County to get shot. If you boys have a party here, let me know."

"You got yourself a deal."

"How about giving me a story?"

"I got one right here, buddy."

He dug in his pack for a manuscript.

"It ain't much," he said. "But it's typed."

"There's only one thing scarier than writing a story."

"What's that?" he said.

"Showing it to somebody."

"I ain't scared."

He walked away. I gathered my papers and headed for the rest room. The English building had a private rest room for male faculty. The very idea of separate facilities had always galled me as a student, and I used that rest room whenever necessary. In the name of equality, I steadfastly refused to enter the private rest room as a professor.

Town people considered themselves above those from the county. People in the hills felt fortunate for not living in town. I grew up on a ridge, and would never dream of living in a hollow, crammed with houses. By the same token, hollow people regarded themselves as better than the wild ridge-runners who lived deep in the hills, farthest from town, roads, and neighbors. Our social pecking order is a Möbius strip, with each group believing themselves superior. Out west I preferred the company of Indians and Chicanos, while in the east I felt comfortable among African-Americans and people from the Caribbean. We were all hillbillies of the soul.

I walked to my office with Eugene's manuscript, seven single-spaced pages on blurry computer printout. It was a sad story with comic elements, about a young man's attempt to get hold of the drug called ecstasy. He was going to college in the mountains, his first time away from home. He hated school and thought of quitting. A series of misadventures ensued as the young man just missed a drug connection or encountered people who weren't familiar with ecstasy. He turned down offers of Valium, Xanax, speed, Prozac, codeine, and Viagra. At every stop he smoked a doobie with other college kids and drank a beer. Finally, frustrated and tired, he purchased some OxyContin, a painkiller given to terminal cancer patients, and snorted it with his buddy. Within an hour his buddy died.

I leaned away from the desk. Substance abuse is a common subject of student stories, but I suspected Eugene's work was based in truth. A number of people in the hills had recently died from recreational use of OxyContin. The protagonist's dissatisfaction with college reminded me of my own anger while a student here. I called the place Morehole, where students were trapped rats with no choice but to eat the cheese. Ostensibly I was living at my parents' house, but they never inquired as to my whereabouts. I owned a four-hundred-dollar car in which I often slept. On cold nights I stayed on the living room floor of a small house rented by two men and a woman. I made a mattress from couch cushions, which tended to slide apart during the night. Sometimes other people slept there, but I always got the cushions because I was a local guy with good drug connections.

If you were the first person awake in the morning you rolled a joint and lit it. You then put the burning end into your mouth, careful to hold your lips away from the fire. You walked through the house and blew smoke directly into each person's face until his eyes opened. We called this "getting shotgunned awake" and considered it a terrific way to begin the day.

Often we cut class and drank beer at the Tunnel Cut, a beautiful spot of mixed hardwood and softwood forest, wildflowers, birds, and water. The area was accessible by a narrow set of ruts, humped in the middle like a long fresh grave. Low tailpipes scraped the ground. We liked to go out there and take acid. We smoked pot to cut the side effects and usually stayed all night, tripping our brains out beneath the stars. We weren't beatniks or hippies, and we weren't punkers or slackers. We were rednecks with dope.

There was a guy among us who preferred heroin to any other drug. He was older than us and had been in the army. His given name was Billy Buck Junior, and if pressed he'd show a crumpled birth certificate, which he carried as proof. Naturally we called him June Bug. He lived in a trailer, one of those tiny ones you hardly see anymore with a bedroom at one end, a living room at the other, and a tiny kitchen in the middle. Louvered windows ran along the sides. June Bug owned a well-stocked arsenal of weapons and ammunition. Eastern Kentucky is a gun culture but June Bug loved his weapons as kin. He carried pistols in lined boxes that reminded me of miniature coffins. He rarely spoke and when he did, his voice was surprisingly mild.

One afternoon June Bug joined us at the Tunnel Cut. He came alone and I watched as he refused the acid we had taken, and quite handily stuck a needle in his arm. I climbed the hill and entered the autumn woods. The sky was a bowl of blue that drenched the world. I could hear bugs crawling on leaves, the snakes and voles burrowing among roots, the bees preparing to sleep through winter. Birds headed south in continuous waves. I was lying amid a four-inch layer of crimson maple leaves with green veins that pulsed in mourning for the branch they'd left. The acid was so pure that I hadn't moved for hours, although it could have been minutes or days.

The first I knew of trouble was the cessation of a guitar that I hadn't even realized was playing until it stopped. Into that void of sound came an automobile heading our way. Most of us then had a terrible dread of cops, whom we regarded as bumbling fools bent on separating honest people from their drugs. That day I didn't care. I wasn't driving and my pockets held nothing illegal. I decided to remain on my back in the woods and move my arms among the leaves, trying to make an angel. The leaves didn't pack right. As I pondered how to give them more weight, I became very cold.

I rose from the earth without moving a muscle. For a long time I examined my skin for goose bumps as a sign of impending chill. The more I looked, the more I saw marvelous beauty among the tiny chips of leaf that spangled my skin like broken gems. My arm was gorgeous. It belonged in a museum, encased within a Plexiglas box on a pedestal of gleaming mahogany. I began experimenting with my fingers, changing their position, seeking the ideal gesture for display. I recognized a momentary time lapse between thought and action. It was extremely quick, but according to my grandfather, nothing was quicker than a double-play, and I began wondering how quick a double-play actually was, while still admiring the astonishing grace of my forearm, feeling the wind against my face like the breath of God, when every sound for miles around was abruptly stopped by a gunshot.

I walked to the tree line and looked down the hill. A stranger lay on his back in the grass, his hand on a pistol. Above him stood June Bug holding a bigger pistol.

All creation seemed to hold itself in abeyance as if time had shifted into reverse, and was straining to catch up with what had not yet happened. The earth ceased its spin. Sunlight became solid in the sky. Fragments of the wind dropped to earth. A brilliant scarlet stain spread across the shirt of the man on the ground.

I don't fully recall the rest of the night. The sun went down, and I headed west along the ridge. I walked ten miles through the woods toward what I hoped was Morehead. The acid was cut with speed, which generated enough false energy that I made it to town. I awoke in the backseat of my car with my face marked by briars, my bad knee swollen from a fall, and bloody scabs on both elbows. I had never felt such thirst. I hurt everywhere.

Slowly and then in a terrible rush, I recalled the preceding day's sequence of events. I wanted someone to steal the car and drive somewhere with me in it. I wanted more of everything but didn't know how to get it. I didn't feel desire so much as hunger. There was life beyond the hills but I was afraid to leave, and my cowardice made me ashamed.

In the ensuing months I quit doing drugs, and stopped hanging around with the old gang. Some people got mad, and others regarded me with suspicion. I tried to act like I didn't care. I never saw June Bug again, though I occasionally ran into the boys who were at the Tunnel Cut that afternoon. No one ever mentioned the shooting. Maybe they were afraid to find out if I knew what had happened. Perhaps the acid interfered with their memory or perhaps I hallucinated the entire incident.

My reverie ended. I was sitting in my office, facing a blank wall. On the desk lay Eugene's story. I read it again, making a few structural suggestions. He was a good writer and I had no idea what to tell him. Stay in point-of-view. Show don't tell. Don't do drugs. Keep away from guns. Stay in school. Always wear a condom. Avoid fried food. Don't smoke cigarettes.

I knew couples who faced pregnancy in college, and few seemed happy about it. I was always grateful to have escaped the situation. If I had fathered a child then, he'd be Eugene's age right now, and what I really wanted to tell him was very simple: Get the hell out of the hills.

Instead, two days later, after class, I returned his manuscript.

"It's a good story," I said. "Has a ring of truth, you know, funny then turns sad."

"Like it could really happen?"

"Yeah. Did it?"

"Sort of. I heard about it."

"How do you OD that fast, Eugene?"

"OxyContin comes in time-release capsules. You take them apart and smash up what's inside, and that takes away the time-release part. When you snort it, it's like ten Percocets."

"Where do they get it at?"

"Usually off their papaw or mamaw who's bad sick."

"Listen, Eugene, I hate to sound like some old man who knows better than you. But drugs are pretty bad."

"I know they are."

"Anymore, writing is like a drug to me."

"I been writing in the woods," he said, "but so far only poetry."

"Good," I said. "Poetry is the backbone of literature."

"Mine sure ain't. It's more like the old busted-up ribs. I was thinking I ort to go deeper in the woods."

"Maybe you should go deeper in your poetry."

"Damn, buddy, you know all the right shit to say, don't you."

"Only about writing, Eugene. Is everything all right up in Martin County with your family and all?"

"Pretty much. Except for my papaw being on cancer medicine."

"Oh, man."

"Just messing with you, Chris. I don't take drugs."

He began laughing and backed into the hallway.

"Your face," he said. "You're too easy, buddy."

I laughed and watched him go, wondering if he was telling the truth. Then I wondered how many times teachers had pondered the same about me.

Arthur Faces Firing Squads

The groups working outside the camp were the main vehicles by which the black market existed. I was in one of those groups, and somebody said, if you get this linen out, you get paid for it. I walked out with those fine linens under my clothes.

We got stopped at the gate and they found the linens. They brought us back to the main assembly. Naturally we had to undress completely. Put all the goodies in front of us to prove that justice is done. All day long we waited in the cold so they can shoot us in front of everybody. This was just naturally what they did. We were standing there from eight in the morning until about four o'clock in the afternoon, and then somebody come by and said, put your clothes on and get out of here.

There was another time with the firing squad, in the main camp at Natzweiler-Struthof in France. Very famous camp for medical experiments on prisoners. We went there in a boxcar. Fifty-two men. Goodness gracious, very comfortable. Lie down, stand up, sit, whatever you want. We had straw and sawdust. They gave us water, they gave us bread, and they closed the car. And they had a hole so we had a potty. The windows were slits with bars in them at the top.

We had bread. I ate two pieces in the morning and two pieces at night. After a while, no more bread. Fourteen days on a boxcar and I am out of bread. I was more than a week without anything. Zero. Finally my neighbor, a gypsy, took a piece of bread, cut it in half, and gave it to me. That gypsy kept me alive. I never saw him again.

We got out of these boxcars at night. It was spring; it was gorgeous. It was the most beautiful night I ever saw. We came to that camp and everybody had to assemble. Just to show us they mean business, they go around and take people for the firing squad. No reason, no rhyme. They picked me and other people and put us in front of everybody. They start shooting. I'm closing my eyes. They stop shooting and I open them. They were shooting over our heads. They said, this should happen to you, you did something wrong.

The third time was in France in a camp. Nicagara, the most beautiful part of the valley. We had no food, so what the cooks used to do, they mowed the grass in front of the barracks and cooked that and fed us. Naturally we don't want to eat grass. We throw it out. They said, look, we know that valuable food is thrown out, so if we find food thrown out, we gonna shoot every tenth one of you. We don't want to have any people dying from hunger here.

We throw out the food and they assemble everyone and they count. I am tenth. All right. I didn't give a shit. We undressed because they want to use the uniform later. They lined us up against a wall, about forty of us against the back side of the latrine. They start shooting. I closed my eyes. Then they stopped and I was still standing there. They shot half the line and I was in the other half.

All I was thinking was: Is it gonna hurt? How is it gonna hurt? I hope it doesn't hurt too long. Ordinarily you have ten guys shooting one guy in a firing squad. But here are two guys shooting twenty. It takes time. They're screaming and yelling because the soldiers don't care if a guy gets hit by one bullet, in the arm or your stomach. He moans, they shoot him again. It's messy. It's not a clean operation.

I took clothing from the heap but it wasn't mine. It was too small and too dirty. Naturally I did not go back for my clothes. I didn't feel like going back and asking for my socks. I hate to wear brown socks with black trousers.

Irene Is Saved Again

In Plaszow there was a Jewish policeman who liked me but I never liked him. So he got his anger ready. He wanted to kill me. He sent me to Scozisco, which is terrible. A lot of people who couldn't work were sent there. It was an ammunition and grenade factory with terrible chemicals. In three months they were dead so they send the weakest people. It saved the trouble of killing them. As soon as we came, we saw people dressed in newspaper with yellow skin from the chemicals.

The supervisor was a nice guy, not SS man. His name was Gajowcgyk. He was *volks-deutsch,* means half German and half Polish. He hated the Polish. He helped the Jews much more than Polish. He said to me, you look intelligent and after the war you will save me because the Germans will lose. You will tell that I helped the Jews.

That's how I got chosen for giving out clean materials. I didn't work with the chemicals and die in three months. He was bringing me food. I was lucky.

Everybody shares a bed with somebody. It's not bad, it was straw and wood. No blankets. My bed partner is Magda and she had typhoid. Spotty typhoid. Very, very bad. If they find out she has typhoid, she go to clinic where she will die. The sick ones were shot. She broke the fever but is like a zombie. She doesn't know where she is. Somebody told me, the best remedy is you hit her very hard in the face from both sides. That's what I did and she opens her eyes like from a dream and says, I hate you. You're really bad to slap me like that. I explain it to her, but she always had resentment. She is the only person I ever hit in my life.

After the war, the Poles find Gajowcgyk and they kill him. I run away because if somebody would see me, they would say, oh, this is the Jew that he helped. So I run to the train, and I disappear from Scozisco.

Brothers of the Hill

Most rural childhoods evolve in isolation, but not mine. In Haldeman twelve boys lived along two ridges connected by paths in the woods. Ricky and Randy were oldest by a few years, then Charley, Marty, Michael, and me. Below us were Roy, Jeff, and Roger of the same age, then Gregory and Faron, and finally Sonny the youngest.

The older boys went off by themselves and threw rocks at us if we tried to join them. Charley was big and quiet. Marty was the smallest and never stopped talking. Michael was tough, I was reckless, and everyone looked after Sonny.

We Haldemaniacs were in each other's homes as much as our own. We rode bicycles along dirt roads, animal paths, and creek beds, flying at top speed through the woods until someone wrecked. On any given day, a couple of us were scraped, bleeding, bruised, limping, and suffering from a black eye or a fat lip. Regardless of weather, we spent every afternoon together, each weekend, and all summer. The woods was our house. Haldeman was our world.

The boys were different now. Every damn one of us had become a grown man with adult problems. One had a heart attack before age forty. Five of us were divorced, three liked to drink, nine had children, two were balding, one was solid gray, and seven were fat. Four lived in trailers and another lived at home. One of us was dead—Michael had used a pistol on himself, and none of us had gotten over it.

After a month I built the courage to visit Michael's grave and stayed there for a long time talking to him. I took a few photographs. He was my best friend, but instead of grief, I was surprised to feel anger. As much as I loved him, he used to piss me off a lot, too. Now, in death, he'd managed to do it once more. He'd have enjoyed that.

Faron had grown into a handsome man nicknamed Hollywood for his resemblance to Nick Nolte. Like many men of the hills, Faron was a man of action, even if that action meant sitting on the porch. He was like a tree with something nervous inside. Roy had gone through the Gulf War and returned with a part of himself concealed. Sonny was learning the trade of plumbing from his father. Randy walked hours alone in the woods. He was the only person from Haldeman who ever sent me a letter. "Hey hillbillie!"

he wrote. "Glad to hear you made it ok. I was somewhat worried as I know from experience that mountain folks don't make good travelers. They usually get homesick before they ever leave."

Roy drove a 1966 Mustang, cherried out, restored until it gleamed in the sun.

Faron drove a yellow Nova that could run like a scalded dog.

Sonny owned a broke-down GTO that he kept beneath a tarp in an open shed up a hollow beside a creek.

My Malibu fit in but the boys were appalled that I didn't know how to work on it. Sonny thought the car was wasted on me and sought to buy it cheap. Faron wanted the double-pump carburetor. Roy eyed my rig carefully. Although his car was easy on the eyes, mine just might be able to outrun his in the quarter-mile.

Some nights we all got together in front of our cars and drank beer, setting the cans on the hood of my Malibu because I had the worst paint job. We lied about the present, reminisced about the past, and utterly ignored the future. We repeated ourselves endlessly. My sons mingled with their kids, throwing Frisbees and footballs and trying to sneak a drink of beer. I was reliving childhood from the other end, but it always ended the same way—arms around each other, staggering in the dirt, wishing Michael were with us, wishing Haldeman was with us, wishing time had halted twenty-five years ago at the apex of innocence. Those evenings were my happiest at home.

Only one exchange comes to mind. Faron had a pistol lying in the front seat of his truck, and I asked why.

"It's like toilet paper," he said.

"What the hell does that mean?"

"I'd rather have it handy than need it."

"Well," I said, "don't wipe your ass with your gun."

"I done did and it went off," Faron said. "You want to take a look?"

"Whatever you do," his brother said. "Don't say yes."

"I tell you what you ort to see," Faron said, "is a old boy's ass I work with. We call him Fencerow. They's four of us. Hogbody's got a body shaped like a hog except with arms and legs like a human. I don't know how Dog Peter Gnat got his name, but we call him Dog Peter Gnat. Now Fencerow, he's the kind of feller likes to moon you when you don't expect it. He don't care. He never wears a belt so he can do it quick. His ass crack is hairy as hell. It's like where a fencerow used to be and the grass still grows thick there. That's why we call him Fencerow, and Chris, you ain't lived till you seen his ass."

Arthur Breaks His Arm

I was working with my friend in Mecarez and we were preparing a factory underground. The Russian prisoners of war were doing the digging, standing in water underground for six, seven hours all day long, day after day. You know what happens to your body when you submerge it in water? You rot away. There was a tremendous amount of dying in those areas.

My friend is in charge of this electrical group and one day he pushed me out. The new situation was much worse. The very nasty Ukrainian SS was in charge. Absolutely brutal. The worst. It was a miserable camp. My friend sent me there. My friend did it to me.

One day a boss comes in. He had an artificial leg. We go into the area where I am in charge of electrical work, maybe six hundred feet down. Everything is dark. Lo and behold, we find my men eating breakfast. The boss chases the men with a stick, the handle of a pick. That's how he walked, because he needed a cane. Everybody ran away but me. I'm in charge. I don't run away. He hits me with the pick in the side. Then he starts hitting me on the head, but I put my hand to protect my head. He could have killed me with one shot, but he was hitting me with compassion, not to kill me. He hit my arm and broke it. My working days are over.

Irene Saves a Boy

Scozisco was a village deep in the woods. They liquidated all the Jews from the village and a little boy sneaked into my barracks. I discovered him very scared. He was too small to work. He would be killed, but he sneaked to the camp to hide. The Jews were completely gone. Nobody wanted him. That little boy covered himself from death.

I said we have to take him out from here because if they catch him, he will be dead. I had this striped dress, it was very wide. And a big coat. I put him under my clothes and he was walking on the other side of the guard. If they catch me, they shoot me. I took him out of barracks to the factory where we work.

I talked to the boss, Gajowcgyk. I told him this little boy

run away from the Germans. So Gajowcgyk said, I keep him here. He can clean my shoes and do the work. He gave him a little straw in the corner and there he was.

His name is Elie Kupiec.

The Best Cake

I talk to Arthur on the phone. He tells me he is lonely. His friends are dead. He is backup man at his temple in order to make a quorum for minyan, and he sees some people then. They are all retired. They look at their lives and examine what they've done with them. One man says he made a million dollars. Another says he made two. Someone else has a yacht and a place in Florida. Arthur claims none of these. He says that he is shrinking.

The cabinet doors of his kitchen no longer bang the top of his head. He spent years walking into the doors from his blind side, then getting angry at his wife for leaving the doors open. At last, he says, old age has made him safe from himself.

Yesterday at the bakery a women cut the line in front of

him but he let it go. The next woman did the same, and he protested. The baker apologized. He hadn't seen Arthur standing there. "Good thing," Arthur says to me, "the baker didn't say I was short."

I laugh at his reference to once having knocked a young man to the floor of a bank for calling him short. The incident happened ten years ago. Arthur told the story with shame and humility, but secret pride. At age seventy he could still take care of himself. Now, at eighty, he cannot. The last time he tried to kneel he was unable to rise. He cannot run and he cannot punch. His bowels treat him unfairly. "Waugh," he says, "it's no fun, this getting old. No fun at all."

The key to understanding Arthur is knowing something of myself. I can never be truly happy because I mourn everything in advance—the wilting of flowers before they bloom, children leaving home, the end of each season during its lovely apex. The same is true of food and sex. Every meal is the finest, which means there will never be another. The last time I made love was the best ever. All further sex will be downhill.

Arthur never thinks something is the best, but that it might be a little better. If he brings home the most delicious cake from the bakery, he worries that there was a tastier one he didn't get. I, on the other hand, worry that there will never be a cake as good. The best cake in the house makes us both sad.

Quite simply, Arthur is adept at surviving rather than living. He knows how to get through a situation. He knows how to circumvent, withstand, compromise. He knows how to hope. He knows how to suffer. It's the living he has trouble with, the same as me.

Arthur looks at the future and I at the past. Perhaps this is why we enjoy each other's company—an unlikely match surely—an eighty-year-old Polish Jew and a forty-year-old Kentucky hillbilly. We recognize in each other what we crave for ourselves.

On the phone last night he was lonely and tired. He is becoming one of the last of his community of Holocaust survivors. He has not made a million dollars or designed great buildings, and doesn't own a yacht. He's not sure what he's done with his life. After sixty years, he still misses his brother.

I get pissed—we are always getting pissed at each other—and I shout into the phone. "You have a successful marriage to one woman all your life. You have two daughters who love you. You have three grandsons who adore you. That is the definition of success, Arthur. Most people don't have any of that. You have it all."

There is a silence on the other end of the phone. He is sitting in his chair in a dim room in Queens, a man who never expected such an outcome to his life—living across the sea from home, listening to a gentile son-in-law shout praise in a foreign language.

"To hell with the yacht," I say.

"What's wrong with a yacht," he says. "You don't want a yacht? Take your family on the ocean. Hire a captain and a cook and lady to massage your neck."

"Arthur," I say, "you should look back on your life with satisfaction. You've done a lot. You're an ethical man and your family loves you. All except one thing—you're short."

"You had to say it!" he yells. "You son of a bitch, you had to say it."

But he is laughing and I know that is partly why he called. I have done my duty. I have restored his dignity with a grave insult. He's still alive, one of the gang, able to take a good joke.

"Good-bye, Sonny," he says. "Good-bye."

The conversation has saddened me. I wonder how I will look at my life when I am in my eighties. I walk through the house to find my sons and wait for them to make me laugh. No one speaks. I realize that they are waiting for me to do the same. This strikes me as funny. I smile. James asks if my face hurts and I tell him no.

"It's killing me," he says. "It's killing me."

Christmas Break

Winter arrives in a slow blur of muffling snow. Each blade of grass leans into its tiny drift. Snowlight glows all day. Squirrel tracks are delicate runes in the whitened earth. I enter the woods, where there is no time, only the slow revolution of season. Winter is the land's long rest, the ashes in which the Phoenix sleeps.

I have gotten through the first semester at MSU. My student evaluations are strong. I didn't forge strong bonds with colleagues but made no enemies either. Teaching four classes a week has left me weary and ready for rest. The house holds a menorah and a Christmas tree. Sam and James are excited that celebrating Hanukkah includes eight days of gifts.

Deep within me lurks a permanent winter, a dark solstice of the soul. Blue shadows spread over the snow like pools of water in white sand. The sky is granite between the hills. I sit in a bare swatch of snow and lie on my back. I want to leave the cuneiform of my body imprinted on the glistening land.

Eugene, my best writer, has dropped out of school. The admissions office has no listing of a phone for him in Martin County. His address is a rural route number. The culture of the hills has reclaimed Eugene as one of its own. I quit MSU twice and I wonder if any of my teachers felt as responsible for me as I do for Eugene. Perhaps I failed him in some way.

It is wrong to play favorites, but every teacher does. I am now left with Sandra, a less talented writer, but more ambitious. The biggest favor I can do is help her transfer to a better school. No one suggested that to me, and for years I wondered why. Now I understand that good students are so rare that a professor wants to keep them for himself.

A sudden gust whirls the air with beads of white like the seed of a dandelion. Landscape is easily understood in winter when the sightlines are open. Without foliage you can see the folds of earth where the ridges dip into a hollow. The initial period following a light snow is ideal for learning the woods because it is impossible to get lost. All you have to do is follow your footprints home.

I have done that but there is no longer any home here,

only what home was. Nevertheless, I am not a fool for coming back. Students seek my counsel when they have difficulty in other classes. One young man drives one hundred thirty miles a day to study fiction writing with me. Junior faculty members have approached me with the idea of beginning inter-disciplinary coursework in Appalachian Studies. There has even been covert talk of an MFA program in Creative Writing, which is nonexistent in Kentucky.

I rise and step into the deeper woods, transformed to a gleaming chandelier of white. Rabbit tracks cross a quilt of snow to a redbud, known in Kentucky as the Judas Tree. During ancient times it bloomed huge and lovely in the woods—white blossoms bigger than magnolias, a sweeter scent than honeysuckle, its trunk more stalwart than stone. The redbud ruled the oldest of the old growth forest. In his moment of desperation and sorrow, Judas hanged himself from the boughs of a redbud. Its limbs became withered and weak overnight. The redbud would never again bear the weight of a man.

I hope that I can forgive myself for Eugene's decision the way the forest forgave the Judas Tree. I am reminded of the old story about the axe that entered the woods. Upon seeing it, the trees said, look, the handle is one of us.

Arthur's Christmas in Camp

Now I am a year in the Nicar Valley. The most beautiful countryside in Germany. The hills are just gorgeous. We have lice and we stink, so they gonna clean us up. On Christmas Eve they told us to disrobe. It's winter and we are standing there cold. During this time they took our clothing and killed all the lice. Then a whole bunch of so-called barbers shaved our bodies.

We had to jump into a vat of Lysol. They sprayed us with something on the head. Then they had showers, ice-cold showers outside. You couldn't walk because the whole thing was ice, the most slippery shit you ever saw. I somehow walked there and I stayed under the shower because the shower was much warmer than the outside air. I stayed as long as I could to warm up.

Finally they brought the clothes back and piled it up in that snowy winter night. Snow was falling all over the place. You didn't feel the cold anymore. People were singing a Christmas song, it was very nice. The next day we didn't work. Christmas.

Irene's Christmas in Camp

We walk in the morning to work in an ammunition factory making bullets. My job was to form a piece of flat metal like a spring and push it inside the bullet. I did this and gave it to another worker. There was a woman guard standing behind us. She didn't beat us. She was not a horrible monster like in other camps.

Some German women are working there, too. They were not prisoners, they were just regular workers, paid workers. When it came Christmas, I think what to do for those German girls. I took this flat piece of metal and I bend it out to make little people they can hang on a tree. I started to produce like there's no tomorrow. I liked to do that. It was nice. You could do many things with the wire. You could twist it in all kind of ways. One day a big SS man came and asks, who takes this metal? This is very dangerous and we need it. Who is stealing it?

I thought this is my last day in that camp. They are going to shoot me on the spot.

He said, somebody is a traitor, doing this. It is a very serious matter. You better tell me who it is or the others will be punished.

So I said that I was not alone but others work with me, too. I want to just make a tree so beautiful. Then the German girls got up and they say she didn't really do anything, we asked her to do it. He liked one of the German girls, so he said he would not do anything. But next time he kills the person who does it.

He didn't do anything to me, because they stood up for me. They had a guilty conscience. I wasn't the best girl in the world. I didn't do it for love. I made those things for food. The German girls gave me food. I wanted food.

A Hollow with Houses

—▬—

Paying late fees on unwatched videos is a fierce gouging in the guts. Each time it happened I swore never again. The old Malibu clung to the tight curves and charged through the dips in the road as I poured the coal to it and arrived at the video store just before closing.

In the parking lot I saw Lena, one of the few girls with whom I was friends in high school. My female friends liked the cool guys who drove cool cars—athletes, outlaws, musicians. The girls dated them but talked to me. I was funny and short, a mascot to their beauty.

Lena had been married twenty-three years and had four kids. She worked as a dental hygienist. Five years ago she moved to Flemingsburg because Morehead got too big.

"It grew so fast," she said, "spreading up the hollows like

floodwater. I wanted to raise my children in a small-town atmosphere. Clearfield used to be separate from Morehead, but now you can't tell where one ends and the other begins. It's nothing to get a bicycle stolen anymore."

"I didn't know that, Lena."

"Morehead's got all the problems of a big town, but none of the advantages. The traffic is terrible, and prices are high as a cat's back. You go to Wal-Mart and don't know a soul."

"But why Flemingsburg," I said. "It's not a town, it's a hollow with houses."

"Oh, Chris," she said, "you still make me laugh. You're just as easy to talk to as ever. Maybe easier."

"Well, I always liked you, Lena."

"How come you never asked me out?"

"I didn't think you'd want me."

"Why do you think I always talked to you so much?"

"I don't know. I didn't think about it."

"You should have," she said.

"I just wanted to get out of here, Lena. The only reason I stayed was failing the army physical."

"The only reason I stayed was I got pregnant."

"Maybe that's why I never asked you out."

We looked at each other, our eyes seeking purchase. The world ceased to exist in time and space. We were fifteen, afraid to kiss. We were twenty-five, young parents working hard. We were thirty-five, both wondering how our lives would be with different choices, pondering an affair with a stranger. We were forty-five and proud grandparents. At fifty-five we quit working and drove a gigantic RV around the country, a gray-haired couple making up for a life spent in one place. At sixty-five, we took walks together, arm-in-arm along the creek. In our seventies one of us died. The other mourned with a gradual withering like a leaf curling into itself before detaching from the limb and becoming part of the loam.

Time swirled back like a tornado, encircling us with the present, holding us fast to the tar of an immense parking lot.

"Lena," I said.

"I know," she said.

I stepped forward and hugged her briefly before turning away. After fifteen steps, I looked back and watched her drive toward Flemingsburg. To me, Morehead's growth meant more things not to do. For Lena there were more people not doing those things.

I drove home to my family, kissed my wife, and wrestled with my kids. We watched a video together. I thought about Lena the whole time. I imagined that she and I were at the old Trail Theatre downtown. I pretended to yawn and stretch, leaving my arm on the back of her seat, and when she didn't mind, I kissed her. It was our first kiss, our only kiss, merely a peck, but it counted—an infinity of first kisses in the darkness expanding through the universe.

At the end of the movie, Rita and I put the kids to sleep and lay in our bed—the same bed where I'd wrestled with my boys, the same bed we'd all four slept in like cats through the cold Montana winters, the same bed Arthur and Irene had given us when Sam was born. I thought of how fortunate I was to have both left the hills and made it back home.

I didn't know that people were constantly inviting Rita to their church. I didn't know that she politely thanked them and explained that she was Jewish. I didn't know that each time this happened, the person's invariable response was, "Oh, I'm sorry."

Arthur's Last Camp

Mosbach is an old city, maybe eight hundred years old. A beautiful German city in the area they call the Black Forest. There is an underground factory and the Allies start bombing raids. I have a show every night. I'm sitting in the window and watching Mosbach being bombed. I'm extremely happy. It's a beautiful night and then you get the airplanes coming. Sirens are ringing air raid and everybody goes into the cellars. I don't mind. I love it. There are rows of bombs going down. The city got hit and everything is burning. We are engaged now in Götterdämmerung.

They missed the factory and hit the city, but there was nothing there. It was just civilian population. We had to clean up the mess, rubble and fires burning and the dead. The men were gone to fight and the old people were already dead. Only women and children were left. It turned my stomach. Women with no arms, babies without heads.

The first time we cleaned up I don't know what to feel, because when I saw the bombs coming I was happy about it. Then I saw the result and I didn't feel any pleasure at all. I could have gone anywhere, I could have escaped, but I wanted to help. I was very happy when somebody was taken out of the rubble. When I found someone dead, I didn't feel so good.

It took a few weeks to clean up, and the people were feeding us. They were grateful. I got butter and milk, things I never thought I would see again. They forgot that we were prisoners of war. They behaved like friends. We did a lot of laughing. We were always joking around. It seemed to me we lived a very normal, crazy life. We were laughing, we were singing. Then they realized that we were Jewish prisoners and they became hostile. They threw things at us. They told us to dig in certain places where there were time-delayed bombs. No more food they give us.

After we clean up, back to the camp. It's peculiar living when you know you're gonna die because you're so sick and there's no medication, and in addition, every so often, the Americans bomb it. We have casualties in the camp and who gives a damn, because we are all dying.

There are guys holding their pants up because all the pants were too big. We call them *Muselmann.* Walking dead. They're still walking, but they're dead already. Just a skeleton. The only thing you see is bones that still walk around somehow. They are holding on to anything to walk.

One night one of the bosses brought in a force of Polish slave labor women. They had bread and potatoes and sausage. You have to give them something for that food. You had to give them sex. The Serbs and Russians, they liked to screw but they had to save their strength for work. So they said to the women, I'll sleep with you on one condition. You give me a nice piece of sausage.

The women lived in France for so long, they thought that we know something about their family. They hadn't seen a man in months. They are doing it for food while getting some news of their husband. It was business, strictly business. Nothing personal. If they are caught, they're dead. And the *Muselmanner* are going back there, holding their pants up, willing to perform sex for food. The Serbs were tops. They could do it any time, anywhere. They brought back the biggest amount of food.

Me, I decided not to shit. I thought that if I kept it longer in me, my body would get more nutrition. I held it until there was no more to get. Then I let it go. There was never much.

Irene Goes to a Better Camp

People were chosen to go to a new place, and I went to Leipzig, a German town that was also an ammunition factory. It wasn't so terrible because they were not killing people on the spot.

Leipzig was very clean, no lice. Terrific camp. Almost not like a concentration, more like a slave-labor camp. A lot of showers for us. It was really more humane. Food was soup and water and bread once a week. But more bread at this camp.

I did a little bit something very sweet in Leipzig. I started to look at a Yugoslavian girl, very sweet. She always smiled when I was passing, so I borrowed from somebody a piece of pencil and paper and I wrote a note to her and I gave it in the hand when she was passing. I wrote, I don't have a family here, but I want you to be my family. And she was writing to me what she was thinking. The same paper and pencil we passed. A half a year we wrote. We never talked. Never. We just wrote the notes. She wrote to me and I wrote to her. I was waiting already, looking forward to when she would give me a note. I never saw her again.

Tilden Hogge and Poppin Rock

Our children attended a grade school with the improbable name of Tilden Hogge. Rita visited the school every day to help with classes in reading and music. Sam and James walked half a mile to catch a bus that carried them ten miles over a narrow winding road known throughout the county for disastrous car wrecks. They spent an hour and a half in transit.

The principal was a former high school football coach who never had a winning season. As sports editor for the school paper, I attended all the games, and sometimes the coach drove me home afterward, long rides through the dark woods. His compensation for a lifetime of county service was command over a grade school. All the teachers were women. They wore dresses to school, because, as one told me, the principal preferred to see them in formal clothes.

One day Sam came home extremely upset. I assumed he'd been in a schoolyard battle and prepared to explain the duality of how fighting is bad but sticking up for yourself is good. I was wrong. He hated school. He was bored and unchallenged. No one was allowed to ask questions. The gym teacher punished kids by refusing to let them drink water or urinate during gym class. Lunch recess lasted fifteen minutes, the only break in seven hours.

I asked Sam if there was anything else.

He shrugged.

"Are you mad about something," I said.

He nodded.

"At me," I asked.

He nodded, staring at the floor.

"It's okay to be mad at me," I said. "But you should tell me why."

He looked at me full on, his eyes damp and scared.

"Because you brought me here," he said.

I hugged him hard, my mind overwhelmed by a crush of memory—years of hating school, the boredom that turned me into a discipline problem, the anger I had at living in a place with no art classes. In twelve years of education, we never had a field trip.

The next day I visited Tilden Hogge to speak with Sam's teacher, and quickly ran afoul of the rules. Parents were not allowed to enter a classroom, even after school. A painted stripe on the floor was a barrier over which no one could cross, similar to minimum security prisons. Talking with a teacher required an advance appointment made through the principal's office.

The next afternoon Rita and I followed procedure and met with the teacher who assured us that Sam was very well behaved and always polite.

"Thank you," I said. "But I'm concerned with his attitude about school in general, not his behavior while he's here. He's a kid who always loved school. This is the first time he didn't."

She was surprised at his unhappiness, and said she couldn't imagine why he would feel that way. She suggested it was due to being a new student.

"He's changed schools before," I said. "He's always adjusted easily."

She told me again how well behaved he was.

"What I'm concerned with," I said, "is that he just doesn't like school anymore. He's always loved learning. I want to try and help him appreciate school again."

She said she thought that was important, and gave us some advanced math workbooks. Rita thanked her and we made an appointment with the principal for the following day. As we drove home, Rita said she didn't think we'd made ourselves clear to the teacher.

"I agree," I said. "It's tricky. I don't want to complain and have her take it out on Sam."

"It's more like you don't want to hurt her feelings."

"You're right. I come back here and I revert or something. I don't want to make waves. Sam is suffering the same way I did. I feel powerless to help him."

The following afternoon we met with the principal in his office. He asked about my siblings. He said he'd read my first book and liked it.

"Thank you," I said. "Sam has always loved school and excelled at it until recently. I'm worried about him."

The principal told us that Sam was a good listener, didn't run in the halls, and had a fine attendance record.

"I'm glad to hear that, but my concern is his loss of enthusiasm. He doesn't like school and doesn't want to go."

The principal said that all kids went through that. He said that I was the same way.

"In high school, yes. But Sam is a third grader. I want to head him off so he doesn't have problems in high school."

The principal asked what problems Sam had at other schools.

"None," I said. "That's the whole deal. He only started having them here."

The principal said that Sam was a model child, and he wished all the kids were as well behaved as he was. He suggested that I work with his teacher on this.

"Okay, thanks for your time. One more thing. I want my boys to be allowed to drink water during gym."

The principal winked at me and said he'd keep an eye on Sam and that I had nothing to worry about.

We left the school numb and frustrated. Rita began to cry in the car. She felt betrayed by local people who'd told us that Tilden Hogge was an excellent school. As it turned out, many teachers in the region sent their children to the few private schools that were available. When I was a child, my own teachers' kids attended Breckenridge, a twelve-year school operated by the university as an enticement to hiring faculty who were concerned about the quality of public schools in Appalachia. Breckenridge was closed now, but some Rowan County teachers put their kids in a Christian academy. Rita and I believed that religion was best taught at home rather than the classroom and neither of us felt qualified to begin home-schooling. We resolved to work with Sam on all manner of outside projects.

A few weeks after Sam's tears, a local newspaper ran a story inviting people to visit an archaeological site at Poppin Rock and help search for artifacts. Some college students had organized an amateur dig, sanctioned by the state, hoping to find evidence of a nineteenth-century town. Sam was very excited about missing a day of school to hang out with cool college kids. Rita decided to join him. She didn't understand why I was so steadfast against going, and I didn't tell her.

When I was a child, I also went to Poppin Rock in the company of a local college student. He had long hair and a beard. We parked on the main road and crossed a fence, trespassing I later learned, and walked through the woods to high cliffs. He pointed to black marks on the rock walls and said they were made by ancient fires. We climbed to a narrow ledge where he gave me a spoon to search the loose dirt for artifacts. I don't recall finding anything, but he discovered the skeletal remains of a baby, which scared him so much that we left in a hurry. He said it was bad luck.

Rita came home from the trip weary and streaked with dirt. Sam was ecstatic. He'd discovered the best item of the day—a hundred-year-old bottle, fully intact. For the first time in months, he was enthusiastic about going to school. He had a story to tell his classmates and a digging tool for show-and-tell. He wanted to be an archaeologist when he grew up.

After supper I read to him in bed. He wondered if you could really dig to China. I asked if he thought a Chinese person could suddenly appear from the earth holding a shovel. He grinned. His eyes closed and I kissed his sleeping face, hoping the ghost of my lips would haunt his days.

A week later an official letter warned me that if my son continued to miss school, legal proceedings would be brought against my family. I made an appointment with the truant officer. Rita wore a dress and I wore a sports coat. We took a clipping from the Ashland paper featuring a photograph of Sam proudly holding his artifact. The truant officer was a pleasant man from the western part of the state who tried to be charming. I introduced myself as a university professor and Rita as a musician who did volunteer work at Tilden Hogge and the public library. The truant officer began talking about "these hill people" and how they required special attention.

"I am one of these hill people," I said. "I grew up in Rowan County. I resent the way you're talking about families you're supposed to be helping."

The truant officer smiled and said that I must miss Breckenridge, the former private school for the children of professors. Closing it was a shame.

"No," I said. "I went to the county schools. Now what can you tell me about this threat from the law?"

If Sam missed any more school, the truant officer was compelled to notify the county attorney, who was in turn compelled to initiate legal proceedings. He said that his hands were tied.

"We're taking him to a museum next week in Lexington," I said. "I've made arrangements for Sam to have a special meeting with a curator. There has to be a way out of this."

The truant officer suggested that providing an excused reason for missing school was one way.

"You mean lie," I said. "You want me to teach my kid that

lying is right." He said nothing. Rita and I stood, bade him good-bye, and politely left the office. Hills surrounded town like the walls of a pit. Eastern Kentucky teachers commonly taught at the same grade school they had attended as a child, as did their teachers before them. Many had graduated from MSU. This insular practice made it hard to stay aware of fresh approaches in the classroom. My difficulties teaching college stemmed from trying to break student patterns that began in grade school, the very patterns that I had been taught. I performed well in school because I excelled at memorization. Teachers gave me excellent grades, in part for making their jobs easier, a method that still held true in the hills.

A recent statewide legislation, the Kentucky Education Reform Act, known as KERA, was designed to improve the schools by breaking down such outdated methods as placing the desks in rows, a discipline originating in nineteenth-century Prussia. KERA was attacked by teachers throughout the hills. Some older teachers preferred to resign their positions rather than conform to higher academic standards. Learning new ways to teach required too much effort. It was not the children who were ignorant, but the teachers. Many were fighting to stay that way.

Having been exposed to more progressive classrooms, Sam could not adapt to the oppressive climate of Kentucky. He said school was like an old movie where the teacher stood in front of the class and lectured, and the students couldn't ask questions. I realized that nothing had changed since I was in school. I had come home to help my people and wound up hurting my son.

Everything Is Simple

No one in my family ever asks about my work. Each book I publish scares them until they read it and feel a certain relief that I didn't tell the worst. I know that Arthur leaves out the worst parts, too. He fears that telling his story might provide fuel to the forces of Holocaust Revisionism who will proclaim him a liar. He believes that nothing can halt the repetition of genocide.

"All the books about the war are full of lies," he says.

"Why, Arthur?"

"When the victims write about their experience, there is a tendency to make themselves sound better than they were. Remember, Sonny, no heroes."

I ask why he agreed to this book, and he says he worries

about it: Did he get the English right? Does he come off like a whining victim? I tell him that no one can dispute the truth. Since he does not think of himself as a victim, he will not be viewed that way. Finally, I assure him that I cut out all his whining.

He chuckles, a brief sound letting me know he recognizes my attempt at humor.

"Last night," he says, "I could not sleep. It disturbed me that my thoughts are on paper. I don't want to say nothing nasty about you, Sonny, but do you understand what I tell you? Maybe I don't use the right words. It makes me feel scared, a strange feeling. I hope you have written my heart."

"I did my best, Arthur. You told your story. That's all anyone can do."

It occurs to me that I am treating Arthur the way my editor deals with me when I call under the grip of prepublication anxiety. Arthur wants to know if I worry about reviews. I dust off the ancient adage and trot it out for his perusal: A good review is helpful, but a bad review is better than no review.

"Besides," I say, "reviews don't matter."

"Sonny," he says, "I think you are lying a little."

"You're right, Arthur. But there's nothing we can do. We have to hope for the best and accept what they say."

"Who reviews books?"

"Very few people make a living at it. Some are professors. Some are writers."

"Other writers review books?"

"It's a way to make extra money. I do it, too."

"Like the Jewish Police."

"What do you mean?"

"In camp they help their friends and hurt their enemies."

"I don't know if it's as simple as that."

"Let me tell you something, Sonny. Something I learned in life. Everything is simple. So simple. Much simpler than you think. Help your friends, hurt your enemies."

"Do you have any enemies?"

"No, Sonny. I have outlived them all."

"Then you've got nothing to worry about."

He says good-bye and hangs up. He's right, of course. The world is a simple place. It is the imagination that makes it complex, and writers are highly imaginative people. Arthur is reacting like a writer with the jitters, but he's not a writer, he's the page on which history was written. Arthur is the book.

Lunch with Alpha Three

The phone rang. I answered and my mother told me that my father would call later and invite me to lunch.

"It would mean a lot," she said.

"Okay. We'll meet in town."

"He wants you to pick him up."

"Okay. Maybe we can eat a late lunch and he can ride back home with you after work."

"He wants you to take him to a place in Carter County. It's his favorite restaurant."

I said okay and hung up the phone. The conversation surprised me because my father has never been interested in spending time with me. He did not visit when I was single in my twenties or married in my thirties. His reasoning was simple: He avoided airplanes due to a leg wound he received while fighting in the army of Genghis Khan. My father was completely serious about being stabbed in another life. It was important that I understand he was not a cavalryman or an officer, but a mere foot soldier.

The only time I remembered seeing my father in a restaurant was the occasion of Arthur and Irene's first visit to Morehead. In a far corner of the restaurant sat a mother with a crying baby. My father stood and pretended to draw a pistol from an imaginary holster. He slowly and deliberately screwed a silencer onto the barrel. He extended his arm, aimed his finger at the baby, and pretended to shoot it three times. He returned the pistol to its invisible holster and continued eating in a casual manner. Arthur and Irene looked at each other and then at their plates. They said nothing for a long time.

No one in my family ever served in the military. My grandfathers came of age between the world wars and I missed Vietnam by four years. I have no uncles. My father suffered a severe asthma attack at his physical for air force induction during the Korean War. He was spared combat and never had asthma again.

The phone rang and I picked it up with the trepidation I always felt when anticipating a call from home. My father's phone manner was a remnant of his salesman days—fake voice pitched low, a bullying cheer that brooked no options.

"I was thinking we'd have lunch today," he said.

"Okay. Can we meet in town?"

"No, that won't suit me. You can pick me up and we'll go to a restaurant in Carter County."

"Okay."

"I want to eat lunch with each of my kids. It might be the last time."

"Okay."

He told me what time to arrive and when I said goodbye, he said cheerio in a British accent copied from television. We'd never shared any private meal together—no breakfast, lunch, supper, snack, coffee at a diner, or milkshake at the drugstore. He saw tomorrow's meal as the last lunch, but I knew it as our only lunch. I felt certain that his insistence meant he had something important to tell me.

Rita was surprised by the phone calls from my parents.

"They want you to drive sixty miles roundtrip for lunch. Why not meet in town?"

"I don't know," I said. "It doesn't matter."

"I don't understand."

"Maybe it'll be a memorable lunch. I hope so."

"You always hope things like that," she said. "What you should do is say something meaningful instead of waiting for your father to."

I drove to town and past the old Trail Theatre. The only other time I remembered being alone with my father was at a movie when I was twelve. I was so excited I could barely talk, and when I did, the words came out in a rush that irritated him immensely. The movie was *Billy Jack.* At the concession stand my father picked candy for me, a kind I didn't like. After the movie we went to the bathroom, and he said that I was an Alpha male. He told me that an Alpha male is more or less the boss dog of any outfit. It meant that pretty women liked to talk to you, and that men naturally looked to you for orders. He said that there were also Beta males, which were plumbers, doctors, and engineers. And below that were Gamma males, which included everyone else. My father assured me that I was an Alpha male. He said that there were three types, and that Billy Jack was an Alpha Two. He waited long enough for me to understand that I was supposed to ask who was an Alpha Three, which I did.

"Me," he said.

The road up the hill to my parents' house was blacktop now instead of dirt, and I remembered that during election years it received a fresh coating of rock dredged from the creek, full of broken glass, old boots, and angry snakes. Walking the woods was much safer than the road. The trees in my parents' yard were taller, and the spreading boughs cast more shade. The edge of the hill had fallen away. As the earth receded, the woods approached like the sea eating away the beach. I wondered how long until the entire hill went over the hill.

My father stepped from the house and I got out of the car. He looked better than he had in years. His face held color and he'd lost weight.

"Barely late," he said.

I nodded. He opened the car door and eased in.

"Seat's too far forward," he said. "Your mother always moves it back for me."

My father adjusted the seat to his comfort, looked out the windshield, and waited. I drove off the hill, following the creek past the bootlegger's old shack, into the foreign territory of Carter County. Charles Manson was from here, although no one will admit it. We passed a famous haunted house, site of poltergeist activity often mentioned in books. Houses jutted from the hillsides, the front porches resting on columns of stacked brick with cardboard pressed into the window frames. Trash filled a creek. Skinny dogs stared at the car.

My father was unusually silent, looking at the road ahead.

"Where's the restaurant?" I said.

"Olive Hill," he said. "A little further."

"What's their specialty?"

"Just lunch. It's a lunch place."

"You must like it a lot."

"Not really. It's almost as close as Morehead, but I don't have to talk to every damn fool in town."

"I thought you liked talking."

"Not while I'm eating with you. We never had lunch together, did we."

"No, this is a first."

"I'm damn glad," he said. He gestured to the car ahead of us. "You can pass this guy if you want to."

"I guess I'll just take it easy."

"That's the difference between you and me, Chris. You don't take as many risks."

I said nothing. We reached Olive Hill and made a few wrong turns and wound up on a dead-end street.

"They've changed the names of the streets," he said.

"You think?"

"How else could I get lost?"

I found the restaurant and parked in the lot. He wanted a different parking space and I moved to it. He told me to lock the door. I said I left the keys in the ignition, and he told me it wasn't a good idea. I said nothing.

We entered the small diner, which contained a Formica bar, a few tables, and a row of booths. I was relieved at the absence of women with babies. My father took a table and the waitress gave us menus.

"Can I help you all?"

"Yes," my father said. "You can give me the name of the architect who designed this booth."

The waitress was confused by this request. My father continued talking.

"He should hang by his thumbs for making this damn thing so uncomfortable."

I chuckled to let the waitress know it was a joke. My father delivered his public laughter, loud enough to attract everyone's attention. The cook poked his head around the corner from the kitchen. I examined the menu. Everything was deep-fried and I ordered an egg sandwich with cole slaw. My father asked for a chicken sandwich. We sipped our coffee, careful to avoid meeting each other's eyes.

"I'm glad you suggested this," I said.

"Yes, a man should eat lunch with his children."

"That's important."

"I've been watching more baseball, too."

"Lunch and TV."

He lowered his voice to a dramatic tone and leaned forward. I listened carefully.

"I want you to know," he said, "that you're the first."

"Okay."

"I haven't eaten with the others yet."

"Well," I said, "thank you."

He leaned back and began to study the decor, which met with his approval. Everything on the wall was devoted to the documentation of a local musician's career. We were seated in the front window and he peered at the lot.

"Your car's still there," he said. "Good thing I picked this booth."

"You bet."

The waitress brought our meal. My father followed her with his eyes as she walked away, then turned to me.

"Your mother and I were virgins when we got married."

The egg was greasy, the toast cold. I took a few bites, then excused myself to the bathroom. I splashed cold water on my face. I lingered long enough for my father to finish his meal. When I was a kid, I would have given anything for this time together. Now, I just wanted to get it over with.

I left the rest room and watched my father from a distance. I had rarely seen him out of the house. It occurred to me that his discomfort in the restaurant was not because of the booth, nor was it due to being with me. He was uneasy at being exposed in the world.

I returned to the table. The waitress brought the check and my father complimented her hair. I paid the bill. We began walking to the door. A man sat by himself in the corner wearing a beat-up hat, dirt on the crown and brim, sweat stains along the band. It was clear that he was simple. My father stopped and spoke.

"That hat is a good-looking hat."

He smiled at the man, whose grin broke light across his face. I opened the door and held it for my father. In the lot, he said, "It's easy to make someone feel good, Chris. I made his day."

We drove home without talking. The meal seemed to satisfy my father. I parked at his house and we left the car. I played football here, raked the leaves, wrestled my brother, mowed the grass. I knew where the jack-in-the-pulpit grew, when lady's slipper bloomed low to the ground.

"Thanks for the invite to lunch," I said.

"You paid."

"I love you."

He nodded. Behind him stood the house I grew up in. I remembered Rita's advice.

"My biggest source of pain," I said, "is the tension between us. I hoped that coming home would help fix it."

"You are quicker to take offense at me than anyone on the planet."

I said nothing. To protest was to prove him right. I hugged him but it was like touching a board. I got in the car. He turned his back. When I honked the horn he did not look toward the sound. His back faded in my rearview mirror—a white-haired man getting smaller and smaller.

While driving home, I thought of a dozen answers to his final comment. Ultimately, though, I was proud of my response—none. I remembered being a teenager in the kitchen and my father handing me a note after an argument. On the paper, he'd written: "Your need to have the last word makes it impossible to talk with you." That sentence is branded forever in my consciousness. To speak was to confirm his point. He had silenced me as surely as cutting out my tongue.

Arthur's Oath of Silence

I have stories by the hundreds. What cruel story you want to hear? I was just thinking that the worst of the whole thing is those people are real people. I survived because someone always fell before me. Very simple. They killed a couple other guys instead of killing me. I owe them and I don't do them justice. I'm telling this story to distill their blood.

I have a tremendous disappointment with my inability to react. Why did I passively endure? There is so much a man can take and then he has to react in order to be called a man. And many times I did not react and I cannot forgive myself for that.

I thought I was divorced from emotionality about it but then I had to relive this thing in order to get my memory going. It's not what they did to me that hurts. It's painful the way I see myself and my weaknesses. I see my mistakes. I should not have done that, I should have done something different. I have to provide myself with excuses. Apparently I wanted life more than anything else. I have two daughters and three grandsons. But in my opinion, they are only excuses. The will to live may be good for the species, but I always thought about myself as a unique individual. I think that's the point, that I am just a number in this. I'm a statistical number. One of the millions of sufferers in this. Every night in camp I prayed to God to let me die in my sleep and every morning I was disappointed when I woke up. That was the most honest prayer I had in my life.

In the barracks, men were killing their wives, and wives were killing their husbands. For instance, a woman would go to a Jewish policeman and say, my husband can't provide me with bread. He didn't provide me with anything. Get him out of here. I want to shack up with you. So the policeman would take him out and kill him.

Every so often the prisoners had to be disinfected because they're full of vermin. The people washed the clothing, shaved the body, cleaned up so they can survive another couple of weeks as workers, because if you are infested, you die. They didn't want to have a complete outbreak of typhoid. They did it on a scheduled basis. All the women would come in and undress in front of everybody.

The Jewish Police were guiding thousands of women to the washing facilities. Right in front of everybody, a mother would say to the policeman, for a piece of bread you can have my daughter.

After the war I see that woman. Do I point an accusing finger on that woman? No. What else should she do? Lie down and die? I said hello, how're you doing, how's your husband? She said, my husband, he bought a new car. I said, what did he buy? She said, it's a Chevy, you know.

What can I tell you, Sonny? This is what you call an oath of silence. We both took it. We all took it, and now I break it.

Bearing Pall

Mrs. Jayne went fast and it was a blessing, but she's still dead and I still miss her. Unbeknownst to me, she had dutifully attended my college graduation twenty years ago, wearing her best church clothes in hundred-degree weather. She waited three hours to see me receive my diploma, except I didn't go. I was already financing my departure by moving refrigerators out of dorms. Mrs. Jayne listened for my name being called without answer.

Today I sat in the front row of church, facing her casket as a pallbearer, and listened to her name being praised. In a jacket pocket I carried my class photo from 1964. Mrs. Jayne stood beneath the schoolroom clock, halted forever at 2:15. After the first day of school, I told my mother that I hoped Mrs. Jayne didn't die of oldness before my brother went to school.

Many years later I sent her a copy of my first book. She told a local newspaper that indeed she'd taught me to write, but that I learned some of the language somewhere else. She said she sat on her breezeway and just stared at the cuss words. She'd heard them, but had never seen them in print. She said she learned to treat them the same as any word. She said that I'd taught her to read, too.

The service was short, the pews filled with her fellow teachers and people from Haldeman she'd taught, many older than me. We carried her out of the church and drove to a small cemetery and lowered the box into the ground. I lingered after everyone left and threw a handful of dirt in the grave. Her name was Mary Alice Calvert Jayne. She taught me to read and write.

I climbed the hill to a dogwood tree behind the small cemetery. All my life I've heard the cross that Jesus bore was made of dogwood, and the tree's punishment was to be forever worthless. The blossom has four white petals with a rust-colored stain at the tip. These marks represent the nails that held Jesus to the wood, turned dark by encrusted blood. People in the hills understand that is why dogwood blooms near Easter. Only the flowers will rise again. Only the dead can reappear.

Relatives held a small reception at Mrs. Jayne's house. They gave me my inheritance—a short lectern made by her brother. She kept it beside her desk. Each child stood in front of the class and read aloud. I drove home and set the lectern in my writing studio beside my desk. On it I placed a massive dictionary. My son James suggested I take the next book I wrote to the graveyard and leave it for Mrs. Jayne's ghost to read. I hugged him and he wiped my eyes.

"It's okay, Daddy," he said. "She's like a grandmaw and they always have to die."

At the end of a visit with Mrs. Jayne, she often gave me a small item to make me feel special. She did it casually, almost as an afterthought, by saying, "Here, slip this in your pocket." She always used the same phrase.

One of her last gifts was a bell, the stationary sort that sits on the reception counter of a roadside motel. Mrs. Jayne kept the bell on her school desk and when the class became too uproarious, she tapped the metal ringer for silence. Hearing it, we sat a little straighter, ready to listen. That bell is on my writing desk today. Its convex surface is dull with corrosion and the base is rusted. I have no desire to clean it. My memories don't sparkle with polish and neither does the bell. I treat it with respect, using it only when necessary. Its clear sound is like a single season compressed. I ring it to clear my mind when I write. I sit straighter and try to focus. I concentrate on the sound as it moves away in waves of time.

Arthur Goes on a Death March

We are in Nicarellis and a man says the Germans are coming to kill everyone in the camp. If you want to run away, there's a train. It was a nice train with benches for the people. I wouldn't have gone in a boxcar. I go for the benches. And here's the joke—three hours later that camp was liberated by the Americans. I volunteered to go to Dachau. Now I have to endure another four weeks of very tough life. All for benches.

I'm sitting on the train and it's dark and I see some red in the sky. Some kind of light. I watch it. I can't move. I don't feel like moving. After a while I lose completely this feeling of time. Days pass or minutes, I don't know. There's no noise, no sound at all. A lot of smoke. I thought it was Hell and everything is on fire, but I'm not hurt. Quiet like

I had never heard such quiet. You have to hear that quiet.

We were caught in a bombing raid. The train is overturned and I am looking through open windows on the side at a burning city. The reason I can't hear is from the bombs. German people pull me out. They gave me a blanket. I remember just a wall of flames and it is Ulm burning.

They give us Red Cross packages and send us to Switzerland. Those packages contain sugar, milk, chocolate, sausages, shortbread, long bread, preserves, bandages, piece of silk, razor blade. All kinds of things I hadn't seen in the last five years. I would have given away my life for it. They took us into the Alps. Beautiful. I suffered in the most beautiful countryside.

The train stops in the night. We hear heavy artillery and know the Americans are in the area. I'm convinced the Germans will shoot us because they cannot let us go into the civilian population of Germany. We might just be a little bit angry. We might not be so nice to the people. If I find out that my wife and my brother are alive, maybe I would not be mad. Otherwise I don't want to live and I have to kill the people first.

The train can't go any farther because the tunnel was bombed by the Americans. Ordinarily we had a lot of guards, heavily armed, but not now. A discussion is going on. They called the chief of the village, and he said, no, you're not gonna shoot anybody here. If you shoot the prisoners, the Americans will shoot everybody in my town. I won't let you do that here.

So lo and behold we walk to the next town. It's the end of April. Snow all over the place. And we are marching through the snow. It is magnificent. The sun is going down and the snow on the mountains is fiery red. We are marching through the night and my feet are very tired. I said in my head, don't fall asleep, because if you fall asleep, you freeze to death. Some of my friends are sitting on the road and fall asleep. The first couple of guys they shoot them. Then they didn't shoot them anymore. They let them freeze to save the ammunition.

I had good shoes at that time and I walk all night long and morning comes, very cold—actually, unbelievably cold. But we walk. I keep myself going. I walk, I walk, I walk. The sun comes up and the Germans are gone. No guards. They left us during the night. We are a whole column of idiots walking alone.

One of the guys is a German prisoner and he knows the area. He said there's nothing ahead, no city anywhere. We have to go back the way we came. So we walk back. No sleep, no food, no coat. We walked all night, now we're going back. We passed hundreds of dead. There were two brothers with us all the time. They wouldn't walk without holding hands and that's the way they fell asleep. They survived the whole war and froze to death holding hands a couple of hours before the war was over. We walked out seven thousand, we came back three thousand. We came back like sheep to the SS.

They corralled us against the river. The valley is very narrow. We're deep in the Alps. The Callevendo. I saw them putting up machine-gun rests.

The German prisoner says we have to get out of here because they gonna shoot us. He gave me a sleeping bag made out of paper covered with tar. I swam the river at night with the help of that German fellow. On the other side, we took our clothes off, we climbed into the sleeping bag because we were wet, put our clothing out to dry, and that was it. I didn't want to get out of the sleeping bag. That night was full of stars, a beautiful starry night. The biggest starry night I ever saw. I slept for three days.

Irene Goes on a Death March

Everything was crashing for the Germans, so they gathered us together in Leipzig. Only Jewish women. A thousand of us. We started to walk on the road. They were shooting everyone who could not make it. We arranged it so three people walk in a row, and the one in the middle was sleeping. We were walking and dragging the middle one, then we exchange places. That's how we sleep. Dragged.

We marched at least a week, day and night. They were throwing us some bread sometimes. Whoever could catch it, ate. I did. I was lucky. They were in a hurry because the Russians were already on the back of them. I had the feeling that we would be killed very soon. It was a long walk and no stopping at night. It was very cold.

The soldiers were talking and I understand German.

They were marching us to the Elbe to drown the whole bunch of us. They didn't want to leave signs of what's happened in the camps. They wanted to drown every one of us.

We march in farm country. There was haystacks, lot of straw. I decided I'd rather let them shoot me than I should walk like this. Me and two others go in the hay. The dogs went all over the place sniffing, but they didn't sniff us. The whole regiment passed by us and they left. It was so silent, the only time it is silent in the war.

First time in my life I decided to run away. The whole time I am in camp, people are pushing me. They said, you go this way, so I go this way. If they want to kill me, they kill me. I am offered, I am here. Do what you want.

We slept in the hay and when we wake we hear Russian soldiers. We came out, holding each other. They give us food, give us a place to sleep like human beings and some clothing. We walked to a train under their protection.

When I come out of the straw, I couldn't believe it. It was something that you can't explain. Can't describe. I can stand up and nobody's killing me. I am alive. It's like the best song or the best music or the best art or the best anything. I am standing there and breathing the free air.

Shrimp and Harley on Foot

Each spring MSU gives a small award to an Appalachian writer. I had been nominated the previous year but members of the English department had protested that my work was of insufficient quality. The last winner had published many mystery novels. This year my supporters prevailed and an award luncheon was scheduled. University protocol required me to include department colleagues, the dean, and any academic alliances that were ready to go public. I departed from convention and invited people from Haldeman, including my childhood buddies Faron and Roy. In forty years we had never seen each other dressed in fancy clothes. Each of us wore a sports jacket, our best jeans with a belt, and shirts with collars and sleeves.

"Goddam, Chris," Faron said, "you look like a Christmas turkey—plumb full of shit."

"Yeah," I said, "and you look like a pup who shit on the porch."

"Well, boys," Roy said, "both of you all look like shit that took a shit."

Many of the people had not seen each other in a while. A few had never been on campus before. I chose a table in the corner near the kitchen, leaving the places of honor for my guests.

The kitchen staff served shrimp cocktail as an appetizer, which I took as a form of culinary flattery. Unfortunately, I am allergic to shellfish and set mine aside to wait for the main course. A few others were doing the same. The staff cleared the table and began bringing sponge cake and coffee.

Rita leaned to me and said, "That's it?"

I glanced around the room at everyone else frowning in hasty conference with their tablemates. I told the kitchen staff that my kids wouldn't eat shrimp and asked for large turkey sandwiches, which I surreptitiously slipped to Faron and Roy.

The president of MSU gave his song and dance about the award and I stepped forward for the five-hundred-dollar check.

"Thank you all for being here," I said. "It has meant a lot

to come home as a teacher because so many teachers have made a big difference in my life. Some of you are here now. One isn't, my favorite teacher, Mary Alice Jayne. She taught me to read. I'd like to donate this check to the Rowan County Public Library in Mrs. Jayne's name. I'd also like to request the money be spent on children's books."

The Haldeman people clapped, their eyes damp. Never before had someone given university money to the county with such alacrity. A few days later Frankie the librarian called me to arrange for official paperwork. She took me in her office, where she told me that she wasn't sure how to handle the check because it was the largest donation the library had ever received. Hearing that, as we say in the hills, just broke my little heart. She said each book would receive a small card pasted in the front that said it was given in the memory of Mary Alice Jayne. She asked if I wanted my name on it and I declined.

I left the library and passed a man walking with a familiar gait. I stopped the car and Harley got in as if he was expecting me.

"Hey, Harley," I said. "Want a ride?"

"No, I just need me a little rest is all."

"Where's your car?"

"I broke up with my girlfriend and the car went, too."

"What happened?"

"Well, she got to where she was wanting me to do things all the time. I couldn't live my life and be with her. Treating her good wasn't enough. Know what I mean?"

"That's why most people break up, Harley. They want to control the other person."

"I had enough of that at home. If I want that, I can go back to the house."

"I know."

"She thinks so much of her own hide, she'd gut herself just to keep it."

"Still not drinking?" I said.

"No, I had me what they call a slip right here lately, but I'm all right now. They said I'm in with a rough bunch, but I don't know no others."

"You know me, Harley."

"You're rough as a cob, Chris."

"You sure I can't run you somewhere?"

"I don't have nowhere to go right now. You reckon they'd let me stay at the jail, you know, for old times' sake?"

"I don't know. It won't be the same sober."

"Damn sure won't, will it?"

"I was thinking of going to Haldeman if you want a ride."

He nodded and we drove east into the hills so steep you'd skin your nose climbing out. With Harley in the car, Haldeman seemed to transform to its former glory. My mind was thankfully free of memory; I only felt our shared past.

"Stand on it, Chris," Harley said. "Let's see what this rig is made of."

I mashed my foot to the gas pedal and held it there. The Malibu jumped forward as if kicked by a giant. Harley was laughing. I forced my attention on driving instead of the land flashing past like speeded-up film. The needle on the speedometer topped a hundred and hovered in the redline with nowhere left to go, but I could hear the big engine continuing to strain. In Haldeman, I slowed for a couple of turns and turned into his hollow. Harley stopped me.

"Best not come up the creek," he said. "They don't know this car."

"Reckon they'll shoot?"

"Can't tell, Chris. If I saw this car I might shoot you for it. It'll flat fly."

He left the car and leaned in the open door.

"One thing, Chris. When you go back, you know, into all that out there. You're still yet a Haldeman boy."

"I know it."

"Keep your ass wiped."

I aimed the Malibu toward town, feeling like a pilgrim in my own country. Haldeman had been abandoned in the name of progress. The feds shut the post office and retired the zip code. The grade school was closed. The only store sat vacant. The roads were blacktop and town water replaced the wells. The bootlegger was gone, the poolroom burnt down, and the poker game moved elsewhere. The steel train rails were peeled from the earth and the cross-ties hauled away. The rail bed was ideal for trailers, which stretched through the hills like cattle cars tethered to the land. Nothing was left of Haldeman except geography.

Time had mown my hometown down.

Everything Is Okay

Each day we taped, Arthur talked for several hours. The sun faded behind the hills and the room became dark. I didn't want to interrupt by suggesting a light. Eventually we sat in utter darkness. The kids were asleep, the house quiet. Arthur wanted to take a drive. We went outside to my car and he stood on the driver's side, befuddled and confused.

"Tell me," he said, "why is this wheel here?"

Relating his story had returned him so firmly to Europe that he expected the steering wheel to be on the opposite side of the car.

"It's okay," I said. "We're in America. It's okay."

"I hate okay," he said. "In this country, everything is okay. I talk to my daughter, she says the baby is okay. Her husband is okay. The new job is okay. Everything is okay but I know nothing. In Europe okay was the first word I learned. They said, do you speak English, and I said, okay. Then I learned fuck you. The next time somebody says something is okay, I'm going to say fuck you."

"Okay."

"Fuck you."

Arthur laughed for a long time.

Swapping Up

My former teacher, Frank Conroy, called to offer a visiting position at The University of Iowa Writers' Workshop. I accepted without hesitation. Rita was ecstatic at the prospect of a return to the only place she'd ever liked living. Eleven years ago, broke and desperate, I'd left Kentucky to attend graduate school in Iowa. Now Iowa was again bailing me out of the hills like my own private French Foreign Legion.

We sold our house within a week, accepting earnest money pending closure. The realtor assured us that the buyer's loan was in the bag. I drove a car held together by duct tape to Iowa City and found a small house in the neighborhood Rita preferred. An Iowa bank granted a loan without my needing to lie, and I quickly closed on the house. Two weeks later, the sale of the house in Kentucky fell through. I suddenly found myself unemployed with no savings, and a quarter of a million dollars in debt. For the next two weeks, I didn't sleep and Rita didn't eat. We could live on credit cards until my Iowa job started, but the salary wouldn't cover two mortgages. Worse, we'd missed the brief window of house-selling in Morehead. The only people who move to Rowan County with intent to purchase a home are professors or doctors, and real estate deals occur for a single month. That month was long past. Our house had sat vacant for a year before we bought it. Now we faced the same problem.

The realtor blamed everything on the buyer, Dale Greer, a man I'd vaguely known years before. He'd had an illustrious career in television before settling in Morehead as a professor. I called him and asked if I could come by and talk. He grunted yes and I drove to his house. He invited me in and we eyed each other warily like two tomcats who might be enemies. I breathed long and deep to ease my way out of the tension.

"Look," I said, "I need to sell my house. I'm in a bad jam. I already bought one in Iowa and now I owe two banks a fortune. When the sale here fell through I had to get what they call a bridge loan and the interest is killing me. Do you want my house or what?"

"Yes," he said. "I want it."

"So what's the problem?"

"You tell me, Chris."

"I don't know, Dale. That's why I'm here. The realtor tells me you're uncooperative, that your loan's no good, that nobody can get along with you."

"That's a laugh. The realtor said you were an asshole."

We stared at each other without speaking. Behind him I could see out the window into a neighbor's yard that appeared vaguely familiar. I recognized the furniture but not the view.

"That's Mary Alice Jayne's house," he said. "I saw you over there before she died. Your kids, too."

"She was a good lady."

"My wife looked in on her once a week."

"The whole county took care of her."

Again we stared at each other. We'd shifted from cats to a couple of dogs trying to get along.

"I should have called you sooner," I said.

"The realtor told me not to talk to you."

"Same here, Dale. I thought maybe you were trying to mess with me on the price."

"I can see how you might think that way, but it's not true."

"That's why we pay a realtor's fee, right? So they'll lie to us about the other guy."

"It doesn't cost them a thing, either."

"No, Dale, we're the ones holding the bag. You want the house, right?"

"I love that house. So does my wife. She's a painter and it's perfect. It's the second marriage for both of us. We're trying to start over. She's from the country and it's a beautiful spot."

"There's some nice woods, Dale. I've made trails in them."

"I know. The realtor showed them to us. My wife is madder about this than I am."

"Mine won't even talk to me."

"Neither will mine."

"What's the holdup on your end?" I said.

"My damn car. I can't sell it. I need the money for the downpayment and what I owe on the car makes me have too high a debt ratio for the loan. It's through the V.A. so I only have to give a small downpayment, but they're sticklers about everything. I'm at the end of my rope. We've run these numbers ten ways from Sunday. It all comes down to the car. Now I'm screwed."

"Me, too, Dale. The realtor didn't show the house to anyone but you, and now the buying period is over."

"This place is a rental. We have to be out by the end of the month. Three weeks."

"We can work this out, Dale. It's just you and me right now. No realtors. I got an idea."

He looked at me hopefully, recognizing the enthusiasm in my voice.

"I'll buy your goddam car," I said.

"Do you have the money?"

"Hell no, I'm broke. But what we can do is write it into the closing contract."

"How's that?"

"I knock the price of the car off the house cost. You give me a check for the original amount, and I write you one for the car."

"It might work," he said. "Sort of like throwing in the car as boot."

"Right, I have to buy a car to sell the house."

Dale called his banker and laid out the deal. I watched his face shift from hope to despair as he listened. His shoulders slumped and he hung up the phone.

"No dice," he said. "The car has to be out of my name before the debt ratio changes. You have to buy it first, but you don't have the money."

"It can work, Dale. We just have to trust each other."

"What do you mean?"

"You transfer the title to me now. I pay you at closing."

"What happens if you wreck it, Chris?"

"I won't."

"But what if you do?"

"I won't drive it, Dale."

"You could turn around and sell it."

"Yes, but if your loan falls through, I'm left owing you money I don't have. Plus I own a car I don't need."

"It might work. We'll add a clause that says if the loan fails the car goes back to me."

"That's a good idea," I said.

"Will you throw in the appliances?"

"What do you mean?"

"I'm putting a car up. What's your boot?"

"All right, stove and refrigerator. But not the washer and dryer."

"Agreed," he said.

We looked each other in the eye and shook hands. Then we went to the courthouse and transferred ownership for a dollar. A year before I had bought the house without stepping inside. Now I was buying a car that I'd never seen. Later his wife drove it home and he handed me the keys. The car had all the hubcaps and a terrific stereo system with six speakers. It wasn't as quick as the Malibu, but handled better. The windows remained in place when you rolled them up. The headlights were bright and all the turn signals worked. If you slammed on the brakes, the car didn't turn sideways in the road. My new Lexus would probably make it to Iowa.

That night, I invited Faron to the house. He parked his massive truck at the top of the drive and swaggered across the yard, his long hair swept over his big shoulders like a Viking. He wore cowboy boots and faded jeans. Faron enjoyed exotic pets such as an ostrich, a wildcat, and elk.

He rode horses in shows and attended the drag strip the next county over.

"About time we got rid of you," he said.

"They offered me a good job and I have to take it—for the kids, you know."

"Yeah, them boys got to be took care of. You'll be back, won't you."

"Faron, I've left here five times. What do you think?"

"You'll be back. Your mistake was not moving to Haldeman this time."

"Maybe we need to start our own Haldeman."

"Haldeman Two," he said.

"Son of Haldeman."

"Shit, that's us, ain't it."

"Damn sure is."

"Chris," he said, "you know what I remember most? The way you rode your bike faster than anybody in the woods. We'd all be setting somewhere and you'd come down the path like a bat out of hell and aim for the littlest space and stand on your brake and just crash into us. You remember that?"

"No, I don't."

"You were the most beat-to-pieces kid on the hill."

"Sometimes I still feel that way."

"Your fingers got so stoved-up it's a wonder you got any left to write your books with."

"I tell you what I remember, Faron. All us boys looking after each other. It didn't matter where we were or what we were up to. All that mattered was we were us."

We looked at each other and rapidly away. We had the past in common, twined memories like fossils lodged in a creekbank. We lacked the language for how we felt. As much as I loved Faron, seeing him made me sad—not at what we'd become, but at what we'd stopped being, innocent children occupying the moment.

"You got a dollar on you?" I said. "Give me a dollar, Faron."

He dutifully pulled forth his wallet, removed a dollar, and passed it to me. I handed him the title to the Malibu, which I'd already signed and dated.

"You just bought yourself a car," I said.

He didn't speak or move. I thought perhaps he didn't understand what I was saying, or considered it a joke.

"Faron," I said, "it's yours."

He still didn't answer. His face showed no expression whatsoever and I wondered if I'd accidentally insulted him. I proffered the title.

"Here, Faron. Take the damn title."

Slowly he reached for the paper, his fingers trembling. He walked away without meeting my eyes. I watched him tow the hot rod off the hill in a drizzling rain. The next morning his girlfriend called and said that Faron parked the car in front of the house and sat in a lawn chair all day, looking at the Malibu. All he did was grin.

I went to the courthouse to pick up the new license plate for the Lexus. On the steps I nodded to a Haldeman boy who was now a lawman. In the hall I nodded to another Haldeman boy waiting to see the judge. My part of the county produced the most outlaws and cops, which made life simpler for everyone.

I waited on a bench for my turn with the clerk. Ahead of me in line were two men in work clothes, clearly brothers, sheepish about being in town. The older one tucked his legs under the bench to conceal his muddy boots. A woman in expensive clothes entered. She obviously shopped in Lexington instead of the mall. The clerk said, "Next," and the woman stepped to the counter. The brothers and I looked at each other. I shrugged. The older man leaned toward me. "Doctor's wife," he said. "Or maybe doctor-teacher," which meant a professor at MSU. I shrugged again.

When it was my turn, I spoke politely with the clerk, whose sister I recalled from high school. The license plate was remarkably expensive.

"Give you twenty bucks," I said. "That's my last offer."

"Can't take it," the clerk said. "They won't let us jew."

Preserving a Name

Arthur calls. Our conversations have stirred his memory.

"A girl went with my mother," he says. "A friend of mine. She died with my parents. She wanted only to help my mother. She didn't have to go but she went and she lost her life. She gave her life for my mother. I didn't, she did. She's supposed to be in the book, Sonny. How could I forget her?"

"You can't remember everything, Arthur."

"There is an old Talmudic story. When God destroyed Sodom and Gomorrah, Abraham said, 'You're going to destroy the whole city?' And God said, 'Show me some good people and I won't destroy the whole world.' So Abraham found some and God didn't destroy the world. That girl, she was one. An angel, Sonny, not a hero."

"You want her in the book?"

"You think you can squeeze her in?"

"You bet."

"She deserves to be. From now on I'm praying for her. Because of you and your book, I go back and back. I have more and more people to pray for. That's all I want to tell you today."

"Okay, Arthur. She's in the book."

"Some names should be preserved. Stella Goclow. Her father was a tie-maker. Very poor. They lived in two rooms. They always had something to eat when you visited their house. She was twenty-five when she . . . when it happened."

"I got it, Arthur. She's in. Her name is preserved."

"Thank you, Sonny. Maybe all this talking is not so bad."

Class Dismissed

I sent a letter of resignation to the chairman of the English Department, who was not sad to see me go. The MSU administration had never supported creative writing, and was planning to have me teach Freshman Comp instead. None of my colleagues said good-bye.

Word of my leaving spread rapidly through the county. No one local was surprised due to twenty years of familiarity with my cycles of departure and return. For a while, my decision fed Morehead's grapevine. I fielded questions constantly.

"I hear you're going out to Hollywood," someone told me. "Be the next George Clooney. He's from over here in Mason County, you know."

"They say you got rich off your books and bought a car so fancy no one can work on it."

"Somebody told me you've got in good with the governor and you're heading up to Frankfort."

"I heard at the video store that the college fired you. They say you ran your mouth like a motorboat."

My response was the same to everyone. I grinned, ducked my head, and said, "Don't reckon."

In private, I had a difficult time with my own feelings—I wanted out of the hills for the sake of my wife and kids, while desperately wanting to stay for myself. I felt supremely comfortable in the woods, but nowhere else. The fact is, I'd essentially failed as a teacher. Most of my work was remedial, even on the graduate level, and I didn't know how to give my students what they required. My chief difficulty was accepting that my students needed to be educated in how to be educated, and I simply wasn't up to the chore. I had long recognized that a colossal problem here was the pervasive sense of shame. Now I felt ashamed for having failed to ease that burden in others.

My impending departure disappointed my students more than anyone but they accepted the news with typical Appalachian fatalism. After class an older student stayed to talk. She was my age, recently divorced, with a son in his twenties. She often missed class because she drove an hour to school and worked half-time out of the county.

"I don't blame you, Chris," she said. "But that's Morehead. If it's something good, it don't last long."

"I tried," I said. "I'm just not sure I did any good."

"You did," she said. "You gave us hope. This school doesn't have a lot of that. These old hills don't either."

"You're a good writer," I said. "Stick with it."

"No one ever told me that before. You're somebody here even if you don't know it."

I nodded, unable to speak. She left and I sat in the classroom until dusk turned the air dark. I was embarrassed by my naïve dreams of return. It now seemed ridiculous that one of my long-term goals had been to run for political office. I felt like a hypocrite for abandoning home so soon. I had followed the historic path of every prior attempt to help the region—VISTA, church groups, the War on Poverty—arriving full of energy and plans, and swiftly becoming overwhelmed by the problems entrenched within the hills.

I clung to my students' disappointment as a balm to my own sense of despair. Perhaps providing hope was better than I had imagined.

Arthur Sleeps in a Bed

I met an American tank column. A Jewish fellow from New York gave me a submachine gun because he recognized that I was a Jewish prisoner. I liked that machine gun. I wanted to feel the metal on me. That was a very nice weapon, very handy. The weapon they shot all those guys with on that hill in Plaszow. Very little recoil. Very well designed.

I walked into a house to get rid of my camp uniform. The potatoes on the stove were warm. Very nice house, beautiful piano in the living room, nice clothing, and a flight jacket. I took the flight jacket, played the piano for a while, took the potatoes, and walked out of the house.

I want someone to talk to because now I'm lonely. Everybody's gone. I don't want to get caught outside. I want to go for the night into a house. I knock on the door and a woman opens it and she told me not to shoot.

I didn't want to shoot anybody. I had just gotten out of prison. I was hungry and cold. I hadn't eaten in days, and I looked like a mess. I smelled. I weighed less than a hundred pounds. I said, could you warm the potatoes for me? I don't want any food from you. Just warm the potatoes for me.

She said she had no coal. She didn't want to let me in, but her daughter lets me in. They gave me a room. The room was warm. I hadn't slept in a bed in five years. They gave me this beautiful room with this beautiful view. But I heard a noise. I said, who's in the cellar? She said, nobody. I want to know what's going on in the house, because I didn't want to go to sleep and get killed. So I opened the door to the cellar, and it was full of German soldiers. They said, please don't shoot.

They had enough of war. And I had enough of war. I didn't know who they were. SS. Army. Air force. I didn't shoot. I closed the door and went to bed prepared to die. I never slept that well in my life.

The next day an ambulance drives me to a makeshift hospital in a beautiful hotel taken over by the Americans. I was dying. Finally I was dying. I waited all that time, but the nurses didn't let me. The Americans brought me back to life.

I wasn't happy. I don't feel good, I'm very weak. I don't

want to go out in the world. I get a doctor to sign that I have TB and I go to a sanatorium. I had a bed for myself. I befriend the doctors, I befriend the nurse. Everything is okay. One problem, I really don't have anything to live for, because I don't think that anybody's alive out of my family.

One day a young boy comes and says are you Arthur Gross?

Yes, I'm Arthur Gross.

Is your wife Irene?

Yes.

Your wife is in Kraków and I came to Germany to look for you. She will be so happy to know that you're alive. I'm going back to Poland to tell her.

That was that boy my wife saved, Elie Kupiec. A couple weeks later, somebody called me from the office. There's a lady waiting for you at the gate. And there she was! She looked very good to me, very good to me. She always looked clean and combed. My beautiful wife.

Irene Finds Arthur

After the war I came to Kraków, looking for Arthur, and there was nobody there. Nobody I know. In ghetto, when I feel like a little unsure of myself, Arthur always said, after the war go to Kraków and we meet. So I did. But no Arthur.

And then somebody like six foot tall approached me and asked me if I know Irene Gross. I said, that's me.

He said, do you remember me?

No.

You saved my life. I would like to repay you.

It was Elie Kupiec, all grown up. No more fitting under the clothes. He went to Germany and came back to Poland and told me Arthur is in a TB sanatorium.

I packed myself and to Arthur I go. I went on a train.

The border we had to go across at Czechoslovakia. The soldiers were watching like they always do. We were walking on the side, away from the soldiers. We cross at night a fence. There was a hole. I was not very physical but I climbed through, somebody was pushing my tush in the back. It was scary. Very scary. The dogs were around and barking like crazy. There was a lot of yelling. Other people were going across and were caught. It was night. We ran until there was a German village and there we stopped. I was twenty-two. Pretty young.

The next day I found Arthur. He was weak like they killed him. He was very good-looking. He still is, but he was really good-looking then.

I showed him my wedding ring. He couldn't believe it. He said, is it the same one?

Yes.

How could you keep it.

I hid it the whole time in the one place a woman has to hide something in.

Waugh, that's why I lost mine. I don't have that place.

Elie I didn't see again. I didn't hear from him, nothing, absolutely nothing. I think he went to Israel, to fight for independence.

Town Is Where You Go

I sent Eugene a letter encouraging him to continue his writing. I also helped Sandra transfer to a better school, or, as she said, "a real school." She appreciated my phone calls and letters on her behalf, telling me it was the most effort any teacher had exerted for her. I was proud until I realized just how minor it was in light of my ambition a few months prior. I told myself that I had tried, but I often wondered if this was true. I'd gotten deeply discouraged and turned tail at the first opportunity. My dreams of home lay in shards.

I made a final trip to town for packing supplies. Snubbing the mall, I drove several miles out of my way to pay higher prices in Morehead, then strolled along the campus. The buildings were the same but several trees were gone, including the tall fir that was decorated every winter with lights. A construction site had replaced the trees with a concrete wall, ramp, and steps leading to a stone gazebo. A maintenance worker I didn't recognize was planting shrubs at the base of the five-foot wall.

"Hey," I said. "What is this thing?"

"Aw, just some bunch of brick we got to take care of."

"What's it supposed to be?"

"Well," he said, "they're a-calling it a bell tower."

"Kind of low for a tower."

"I'd say so," he said, "but I ain't never seen a real one. Maybe some come low."

"Where's the bell?"

"They ain't no bell. They got speakers. Supposed to be loud ones."

"Well," I said.

"This whole thing run a million dollars. Some rich lady from Lexington gave the money."

"For a bell that don't work."

"Yup." The man grinned. "And a short tower."

"Didn't anybody say something about chopping all the trees down?"

"They put us to doing it when the students were gone. They was some to get upset, but it didn't do no good. You can't put back a tree."

"You sure as hell can't."

"I'll thank you not to talk that way."

"What?"

"Bad language and such."

"Sorry," I said. "See you."

He nodded and I continued my walk, his request a reminder of where I was—not merely in the Bible Belt, but smack dab in the middle of its giant buckle. I was going to miss the woods, but not the constant self-oppression.

There is a children's model that you assemble with glue called The Visible Man, a transparent shell containing the organs of a human. As I walked the crooked Main Street, I felt as if my body was exposed, my nervous system raw to the wind, my heart on view. Only my mind remained hidden. I was The Visible Ghost, recognized by people I knew twenty years ago, ignored by everyone else.

My favorite spot in town was on the courthouse lawn, sitting behind a monument that honored fallen soldiers. A statue of a doughboy strode through a jumble of barbed wire. He was perpetually heading east toward the hills that hemmed the town. Fastened to the base of the statue was a list of fallen soldiers, their last names as familiar as the sound of rain. It was hometowns that enraptured me with awe—Hilda, Craney, Yale, Smile—names I had never heard. Where in Rowan County was the community of Smile? Eventually people wouldn't know where Haldeman was. They will study a map or a plaque or a book and find a reference to a town that no longer exists. My hometown will be a land of ghosts.

See what the town is, I told myself, not what it was. I opened my notebook and dutifully recorded what appeared before me. The paint on Progress Hall was peeling. Battson's was a pizza joint, the courthouse was a tourist attraction, and the old jail was used for city storage. Behind it, a manhole cover had been seeping raw sewage into the street for two months. Cars drove through it and people walked in it. Directly above it hung a sign welcoming parents to Morehead State University.

Suddenly a voice yelled at me.

"You writing a book?"

I recognized a boy from childhood who had inexplicably become a grown man driving a huge truck.

"You bet," I said.

"I thought that's what you was up to."

"You want to be in it?"

"Hell, yes," he said. "I'll give you a beer."

"All right. You're in."

"Write me a whole chapter and you can have a shot at my old lady. But it ain't as good as everybody says."

I laughed and the light changed.

"See you, buddy," he shouted, and drove away.

I left the statue and walked half a block to visit the

library. Frankie was gone and I wrote her a note. As I was leaving, my seventh-grade teacher pushed open the heavy doors. Mr. Ellington seemed extremely tall when I was a kid; now he appeared to have shrunk. As the only male teacher at Haldeman School, he enjoyed special status as auxiliary bus driver, stern disciplinarian, and favored teacher of the boys. He brought enough pocket knives for each boy to have one, then showed us how to carve soap. Sometimes students gave Mr. Ellington broken guns that he repaired at home.

One day each year he came to school wearing a buckskin shirt and leggings he made from a deer he'd shot. From his belt hung a powderhorn, a bullet pouch, and a leather bag containing flint and wadding. He also carried a Bowie knife and a tomahawk, which he could throw with remarkable accuracy. He fired his long rifle out the classroom window so we could see the twin puffs of smoke—one from the powder igniting in the pan, and the second billowing from the muzzle.

"Mr. Ellington," I said. "Is that you?"

He nodded, staring hard at my face, trying to place me amid forty years of children exchanging places in his classroom.

"I'm Chris Offutt," I said. "From Haldeman."

"Chris," he said. "How are you getting along? I heard you were in."

"That's right."

"I'm here every day. I mainly read Louis L'Amour."

"I've read him."

"Would you like to see my pride and joy?"

I nodded and he opened his wallet. I expected to see a sports car because he had the reputation of a leadfoot. Instead he pulled out a color photograph of a bottle of the dishwasher fluid Pride, beside a bottle of the detergent Joy. He chuckled, holding the thin bridge of his nose between a long bony forefinger and thumb, a familiar gesture.

"Take that with you," he said, handing me the photograph. "I'm the champion horseshoe thrower in the state in my age group. Over seventy. Say hello to your brother and sisters."

"Your Kentucky history class had a big effect on me. You were a good teacher."

"I read your books," he said. "You wrote it the way it is, not the way some people wish it was."

He walked past me, surprising me with the suddenness of his departure and the agility in his step. I had often imagined that if calamity befell my parents Mr. Ellington would adopt me. He'd raise me as the son he never had and teach me how to make moccasins, load the long rifle at a run while dragging the gun butt behind me in the brush, throw a tomahawk, sharpen a knife, cut a fishing pole and make a hook, survive in the woods on game and wild vegetables, start a fire with flint, and live in a rockhouse.

I went outside and blinked. Mr. Ellington loved Kentucky heritage, and conveyed a certain pride to all his students. More than anyone, he showed us who we were in the hills. History itself is accomplishment, and he had displayed ours. Mr. Ellington gave us identity by giving us himself.

I studied the contour of the hills against the sky and realized that I had been mistaken. Eastern Kentucky did have heroes after all. Mr. Ellington was one.

Unleashing History

I finished the first draft at two in the morning and collapsed in bed. Rita read it until five A.M. then woke me to discuss it. At seven she went to bed while I got the boys fed and dressed and off to school.

Since reading the manuscript three days ago, Rita has been profoundly depressed. She can't sleep. She cries daily. She is volatile with the kids and me. Arthur had never related his war experiences. Irene had told them vaguely, often as bedtime stories for Rita, presenting her incarceration in a glowing light.

Today I suggest we go for lunch and Rita dresses up, unusual for her. I drive to a restaurant but she begins to cry and refuses to leave the car. At home, she crawls into bed and continues crying. I bring her a cup of tea, which she refuses to drink. After several hours of her tears, I have no choice but to call Arthur.

"I need your help," I say.

"Uh oh. What's wrong?"

"Rita read the book. It upset her because she didn't know what happened to you."

"Waugh, I didn't advertise it."

"I know, Arthur. I understand. The thing is, Rita is upset. She's really upset, Arthur."

"You want I should talk to her?"

"Maybe you can tell her it wasn't as bad as you made it sound."

"It wasn't, Sonny."

"No?"

"Much worse. Much much worse. You received the highlights only."

"Don't tell her that."

"Let me talk to my daughter."

I give the phone to Rita in bed. I try to comfort Sam and James, who are worried about their mother. They have never seen her behave this way and decide it is their fault. I assure them otherwise. The fault is mine, I realize. I have unleashed history on my own family, attacked my wife with the past. I am to blame for her misery.

I hear Rita say into the phone, "No, Daddy, it's not your fault."

Sam and James are making cards for Rita. The bold letters say "I love you. I'm sorry."

It occurs to me that herein lies the problem: We all feel guilt, we are all to blame. The Holocaust is humanity's tender scar. Everyone is sorry—the Jews, the Germans, all of Europe and America. Even my children feel the scalding of the past without knowing where the burn comes from.

Arthur's War Is Over

They took me to another hospital in Ferdafink, Bavaria. I'm in a sick bay in a refugee camp. Now it's more or less a month after the war. In the meantime, my friends are out there, doing things, collecting things, robbing things, shooting people. Everybody takes whatever is left of Germany.

Some of the electricians I work with found out that I'm in this hospital so they came visiting me. They said, we have a present for you downstairs. I go downstairs with them. They brought the guy who broke my arm. They had beat him up and bound him to a dolly, beat him up a little more, and brought the dolly to me. So I see this piece of flesh, it looks like a bunch of shit. I said, get him out of here, will you? I'm not interested. I got very mad. My friends thought it was cute. Not me. The war is over. My war is over.

Irene Won't Steal Clothes

Ferdafink was the place where refugees lived for a while. It was a Hitler Youth Camp that we take over. I didn't have any clothing. Many people were going into the houses and saying, you are a German and I'm a Jew and I suffered, so you give me clothes. They were stealing clothes but I didn't want that.

What I did, I took a blanket of the German army and made it an outfit. Many of the Jewish girls were rather heavy and short and they would not wear a blanket because they would not look so good. I was slim, I was tall. It's warm and I don't have clothing. I'm not going to steal anybody's clothes.

In the refugee camp, a policeman started to attack me with hate. He said to Arthur, what are you doing with that

German bitch? So Arthur knocked him down. They put Arthur in jail and I had some friends in Ferdafink and they got him out.

I am never far from Arthur since the Liberation. Even now. Never far.

Burying an Owl

I rise with the birds and step into the silky light of dawn. The sky is an old chalkboard in need of a wash. Morning mist lends a fragility to the land, as if the woods are draped with lace. The woods are heavy with summer, each leaf burdened by the weight of life. A rotten log breaks like cake beneath my boots. Landscape is imprinted in me with such ferocity that my very marrow is made of earth.

A great horned owl has lain in my refrigerator for six months since I found it on the interstate last fall. It was by the road, one wing aimed up like a tombstone to flight. The bird is eighteen inches tall with a wingspan of nearly three feet. The plumage is golden brown. Its tail feathers are stiff and strong, acting as a rudder for soundless travel. The claws are big as my hands, its beak as sharp as a blade.

The owl's head wears the tufted feathers that give it a name. Native Americans consider owls bad luck. Ancient Egyptians thought they were good luck. To the Babylonians, hooting owls were the ghosts of women who died in childbirth, calling for their babies.

Fog turns the air white between the trees. Distant foliage is hidden as if by scrim. It is the varied sounds of the woods I will miss the most—leaves in wind, the rise and fall of distant locust, a jarfly's rattle, the frogs at night, birds at dawn, the sharp sound of a stick snapping in cold air.

Owls are the only bird whose eyes face forward. They roam at night. They are big and loud, but kill in swift silence. Owls are so much like humans that we are afraid of them. A sudden rain spatters the woods, making a steady sound like a creek inside a cave. Distant trees are grayed by mist. A dead bird is in my arms.

I am tampering with the natural order since no crows will peck the remains, insects won't nest in its hollow bones. We have killed the owl's only predator, the big cats, and now we are limiting its habitat. Owls fly along creeks. They do not understand bridges and an owl will often shatter its neck against the side of a truck. I have buried seven such owls around the country. They visit me in my dreams.

I hold the owl close to my chest to shelter it from rain. A terrible brush with man took its life, and its final touch should be one of kindness. I dig a hole and gently place the owl inside the walls of earth. I fill the space, set a rock on the dirt, and sprinkle last fall's leaves over it. There is nothing to be said.

Everything I own is stacked in boxes. I look at the woods and want to remain. The owl lies below humped earth at my feet. I am saying good-bye.

Arthur Thinks of Home

Home is a feeling, nothing more. Home is illusory, like love, then it disappears. Once you leave, you become a stranger. I lost my home and that's forever. I wouldn't go back to Poland. It breaks my heart. They don't want me there. All my memories are shadows, lousy shadows. That country is forsaken. Home is where I hang my head.

Epilogue

The truck is packed. The house is sold. The trees don't care. These woods were never mine, they just lent themselves awhile. No one can ever truly own the woods any more than you can own another's thoughts. Today my dream is to know the mind of a tree.

To that end I hereby decree that I will be buried in a pine box with an acorn in my mouth. An oak will grow from my head, pressing its roots like flowers within my ribs, piercing my skull and slithering deep into the earth. I want my boughs to shelter children a hundred years from now. I want to be a tree where pilgrims trek for knowledge. I want lovers to caress each other in the soft ground beneath my shade. I want to withstand snow and wind, rain and drought, fire and hail. I want to thrive in the woods and die in the woods, return to the woods and become born in the woods.

I want to stay home.

I am ready to leave.